THE SECRET LIVES OF PEOPLE™

Real Diary Excerpts from Modern Day America

By L.M. Hughes

http://www.thesecretlivesofpeople.com

ISBN 978-0-9888417-1-0

Dedication

This book is for all the wonderful women who were brave and generous enough to share their deeply personal stories with the world. I admire each and every one of them for being so open and for submitting their journal entries to me despite any fears they may have had of judgment from those who have not walked in their shoes. Thank you all so much for sharing your hearts and souls with me and everyone else who is privileged enough to read about your private lives. You all seriously rock!

In addition to being extremely grateful to the many anonymous authors who were so brave to share intimate details from their lives, I'd like to extend many thanks to the following authors who contributed excerpts to the book and did not wish to remain unidentified:

- Joni Carlo
- Tiffany A. Miller
- Deb Johnsen
- Samantha Edwards
- Calliope Katamathēsis
- Annie DeWit
- R.E.S Tidmore
- Mary White

http://www.thesecretlivesofpeople.com

Table of Contents

http://www.thesecretlivesofpeople.com

http://www.thesecretlivesofpeople.com

Introduction

I got the idea for this book from a dream I had shortly before Christmas in December 2011. In my dream I had swapped pages of my diary with a friend. When my friend returned my diary excerpt, she had ripped up the pages because it was so scandalous and personal, and she figured it would be best to rip it up to protect me from the chance that someone would ever read it and "find out about me."

I knew immediately when I woke up that the dream came from two real-life experiences that I had. The first was when I left my diary out on my bed as a teenager, after which my father found it and read about, in great detail, how I performed oral sex on a guy. I was so embarrassed and humiliated! The second real-life experience was when I was 34 years old or so. I went into my back yard and found a pile of dirt in my unplanted garden bed, and ritualistically tore out the pages of my diary and burned most of it. I know, burning your diary might seem crazy and a little extreme, but the purpose of this ritual was to try to release and dispose of all of the negativity contained in those pages – to set myself free. I was determined to let go of the pain inside me that had been caused by my numerous failed relationships, and this was the best way I could think of to create a shift in consciousness for myself and release the sadness I had felt about not having found a partner in life.

I had the dream right around the same time that "Fifty Shades of Grey" by E.L. James was starting to gain popularity, and I had an epiphany to write my own best-selling book. I was so excited after waking up from the dream and knew that a collection of diary

http://www.thesecretlivesofpeople.com

excerpts would be the type of book that many people would want to read, because it was the type of book I'd want to read!

I think we've all fantasized about reading someone's diary at some point in our lives, or have maybe even rifled through one as a parent checking on their child or as a roommate who gives into a temptation that's just too strong to resist. It's just normal to want to know someone's secrets, and be curious about who they really are or how they really feel about people or events. To know someone else's secrets helps us answer our own question, "Am I normal?"

Even though I think it's a terrible invasion of privacy to read someone's diary without permission, as my father did when I was a teenager, it's a normal human instinct to do so if presented the opportunity. With the way that consumerism encourages us to form an emotional connection with products instead of people, we seem to be increasingly disconnected from each other. Because of consumerism's pervasive influence over our media, and the subsequently skewed portrayal of "regular" people, it's more and more difficult to know what's normal. I think people want to explore deep emotional issues, but without the fear of judgment from others, and that's tough in the real world – at least in America. Just look at any talk show guest who has crossed, or even simply been accused of crossing, a line of social propriety. They are typically judged very harshly by their audience. This book provides the anonymity for people to put everything out there uncensored.

Since I knew that the idea for this book would be very intriguing to many people, I went from dreaming about it to posting an ad on www.craigslist.org. I was looking for people with an innate ability to make people laugh or cry with their writing, and who were able to be vulnerable and/or inspire people. I wanted writers who were willing to be open and honest about all of the embarrassing, funny, painful, weird, or sad experiences they'd had, and who had chronicled those experiences in their journal. Regardless of whether the topic was sex, parenting, loss, illness, or everyday life, I had everyone who submitted their journal entries sign a confidentially statement so that their identities would be protected. Names have been changed throughout the book to protect people's identities. Of course, since people do not censor themselves in their journals, I did not restrict the content, and I made only minor edits to the content to preserve the authenticity of the excerpts. Therefore, you might notice spelling or grammatical errors.

Readers should be aware that sensitive subjects, controversial and/or sexual topics, and foul language were NOT excluded from this book. I hope that readers will take care to protect minors from reading the explicit adult material contained in this book.

You might ask, "What's in it for the authors? Why would they put themselves out there to the world?" This is my authors' opportunity to be understood, to connect with people, and to potentially even make a difference in the world through their writing. Of course, people usually write in their journal mainly during difficult times, so many of the "stories" are emotionally tough to read. I freely admit that I cried when I read some of them. It's probably therapeutic for my authors to release some of the pain by sharing their story with someone else, even if it is a complete stranger. At least the feelings are not held inside anymore. I'm sure the authors' biggest hope is that the readers will learn something from their mistakes.

The benefit of reading this book is that you just may realize that someone else has had a similar experience to your own or you may realize that you have a lot to be thankful for after reading about the struggles that many of my authors have gone through.

http://www.thesecretlivesofpeople.com

You might even get a good laugh at some of the more light-hearted material. Either way, I really hope that anyone who reads this book will withhold judgment and simply be grateful that they got to glimpse into someone else's deeply personal experience. I hope you enjoy the rare opportunity to read about The Secret Lives of People.

If you'd like to submit your own journal excerpt for consideration in the next book of the Secret Lives series, please visit http://www.thesecretlivesofpeople.com for details.

Excerpt One

06.10.2005

Part of me died today. A part I don't think I'll ever get back! You hear Oprah say shit about your defining moments. You know- the ones that change everything. I thought it was a croc until now. I'm eating my words and they're tough to swallow.

When the letter came in the mail for Dusty today, I was so excited. He was going to be so happy. A letter from Dad, how great!

Wrong.

This was Dusty's first time dealing with a deployment. Well, the first deployment he'd remember that is. The last one he was only a baby. Sigh...my heart aches just thinking about it.

Anyhow, I called Dusty into the dining room where I'd been working. He sauntered into the room not sure why I'd called him. Round hazel eyes, wide in question, stared up at me. I slapped the letter in his little hand. He looked down at his palm and at the handwriting on the envelope. He squealed with joy like a little piggy, "Dad!" He tore open the envelope. I laughed at his enthusiasm. It was good to see him so happy. The last few weeks without his dad, his hero, was wearing on him. It was making me worry.

I asked him if he would read it to me. He plopped down right there on the floor cross legged and tossed the envelope aside. I followed suit.

He began. "Dear Buckshot," he read with a giggle. His pet name from his dad and grandpa. "I hope you're being a good boy for your mom." He looked at me and winked. Who would've thought, the kid was only five.

He was taking his role as man of the house very seriously.

But then something happened. Something that changed us both.

Dusty spoke quietly, then stopped altogether. I thought maybe he couldn't read a word. So I asked him to sound it out. He shook his head. His chest heaving, I looked at his sad face. Tears sailed down his full cheeks. A lump instantly formed in my throat. My little man was hurting and I didn't know why. I asked him what was wrong. He clutched the letter in his small fingers.

"Daddy's not going to be here to watch me play soccer, is he momma? He's not going to see sissy (his sister Kaitlyn) walking around crying for him, is he momma?"

Hot tears burned my eyes. My heart tore down the center. I wanted to lie to him. To tell him daddy would be home soon, but I wouldn't do that to him. I wouldn't give him false hope. It was the worst thing you could do to a child in a military family. Always the truth. No matter what.

I shook my head trying to find a way to speak around the lump in my throat. "No baby, he's not!"

Dusty choked back a sob. At five years old I saw the little soldier within. He tried to get control of the pain on his perfect face. But it was too much. The hurt was too deep. He clung to the letter and began rocking back and forth. He sobbed whole heartedly. I wrapped my arms around him and held him as tight as I could, desperate to lend him my strength. He sank into me. I placed my cheek on his blond head. There in the middle of the dining room holding each other, he cried for the absence of his father and I cried for the piece of innocence that I stole from him. I wanted to find a way to save that piece of him and take away the pain that tore at my little man's heart. But I couldn't, I was helpless. Helpless. I cried and cried. What had I done?

I chose to be a military wife. Dusty wasn't given a choice and neither was Kaitlyn, only two and a half. Blake and I together stole a piece of our son and I feared soon our daughter. We put Dusty through pain many other children will never face. I think when you marry a military man or woman you tell yourself I can do this. That somehow you'll be strong enough to survive. But then comes a day like today and you think. Maybe I was wrong. Maybe I can't do this and maybe my kids shouldn't have to do this either. So what now? What do I do now?

Kaitlyn heard Dusty crying and she'd come running with her pink blanket she called "ME" dragging behind her. She didn't know what the problem was, but her little amber eyes filled with tears. Her bottom lip popped out and quivered. "Dusty crying, mommy," she said in her little voice pointing to her brother. And tears fell from her eyes. She knew if momma and brother were crying she should be crying too. I pulled her into my embrace with Dusty and together we cried.

It was that moment I truly knew I wasn't in this deployment alone. People try and support you, but the truth is, it is not directly affecting their life. They cannot fully understand the weight of the pain you carry in your heart.

Author's Note:

This was my husband's second deployment after we'd been married. Lucky for me, he'd already served five years overseas in Japan. Making my navy wife career 15 years instead of 20. When my husband Blake was deployed for the first time after we were married, I was 19 and five months pregnant. As you can guess I gave birth to my first son alone. Though at the time it was hard on me, it was nothing compared to this day and this deployment. This deployment took place after Bush declared war against terrorism.

My husband left for a six month deployment that turned into a nine month deployment.

This day changed me and how I thought about military family life. You can't think of only you when marrying a military man. You have to think about your unborn children and if this is a life you want to give them.

Excerpt Two

April 2012

"What's it like to be a grown-up?" she asked.

A 7-year old.

Hmmm. So, how can I answer this without ruining her forever? How can I put it in terms a person who's only been around the sun 7 times can understand? We were just talking after school, she and I, while her dad went next door to help the neighbor. I figure I might as well ask her some questions before she gets to be a pre-teen and hates talking to adults, or at the very least, hates talking about school to adults… [I recently heard that one question kids hate is 'how is school?' and who can blame them… it's just that adults don't really know how to make conversation. Let's suffice it to say, different interests.] At any rate, we already went through the school conversation, which by the way, she was very into having. We did this and that and this and that… it was so cute, actually.

Then she threw a curve ball at me…. "What's it like to be a grown up?"

About 100 thoughts went through my head in that moment. Everyone will answer this differently. What can I say? What will she understand? Don't give too much info, but don't give not enough info!

At any rate…I really don't recall what I told her… I think it was not a great answer, it was kind of lame. It included the word "complicated"… sadly… oh well… My response also included "ask every grown-up you know and you will get a different answer. Your mom and dad would each answer that question totally differently, for example"… anyways.

~15~

I also knew the moment she asked me that I would be contemplating that question for days. And sure enough, so far so good... I like my friend's answer: you get to eat ice-cream for dinner! So true.

The good: you get to eat ice cream for dinner. You get to do what you want when you want. You get to stay up late and no one tells you not to. You get to sleep in if you want, sometimes. You get to have sex! With whoever you want! You get to do all sorts of stuff!

And the bad: you get to buy the ice-cream that you eat for dinner. You get to hopefully, have a job and work for a living. You get to pay bills and do all sorts of things like that. You get to get STD's from all that sex! Or get pregnant! You get to have way more responsibility than you wanted to, possibly.

The 'in-the-middle': you get to have sex, did I mention that already? You get to do drugs. You get to make your own decisions. You get the consequences of your decisions, both positive and negative. You get to buy a home, maybe. You get to choose your clothes, your style, your things, your places. You get to choose your friends. You get to choose a spouse, or a relationship. You get to take care of your older siblings, and maybe as they age, your parents. You get to prepare the holiday meals. You get to host the parties. You get to clean up after the parties. You get to go on vacation, maybe. You get to pay for the vacation. You get to comfort the scared kids... but you get to feel bad for them too, cuz you know it's okay but they just don't yet.

I'm not sure if being a 'grown-up' is all it's cracked up to be, really. I mean, it sounds quite finite when we use that word. Like, done! I'm all grown up now. Finished.

Hmph.

But it's certainly a work in progress... at the very least.

It reminds me of when I was about 15 I thought that I'd have "it" all figured out by the time I was about 24 or 25…graduated from college, I'd be smart, about to get married, and then get ready to have some kids. And I'd know how to solve my own problems and be spiritually aware and I'd have all the answers that my biology teacher posed to us in high school.

Then as I turned 24, and then 25, and then 28… I had to think about that 15-year-old-me and just laugh my head off. Because of course I didn't have it all together and I certainly did not have the answers to my biology teachers' questions. And I thought I'd be married and 'settling into' a family and a husband. Ha ha! No way! Not after I found out how much fun it was to be promiscuous and have sex with a bunch of different people… men and women. Both are fun. ☺

Then in my 30's… same thing. Life was just fun. And I sure as hell wasn't done as a grown-up. It was not finite. But I was definitely getting closer –in my opinion- to the types of life-long Buddha Tao contemplative questions that my biology teacher posed way back when. And I became happy… well, content, for the most part, with who I was… and who I am. Not to say I'm not fucked up in some ways, but I definitely was more together than the 24 or 25 year old me. By. Far.

[Thank. God. And that is literal.]

And now? Another almost-decade later? Knowing you don't have all the answers is I guess good. And being more patient about things, is good. And slowing down? Not so good. Not so fun. I don't have a parameter for what I 'should' feel like. But I watch the 7 year old play and I know I do not –in the least- have her energy. Ugh. ☹ and I'm not super happy about that. But, yet, people I know often tell me that I'm "so energetic!" Wheee!!!

And I definitely know that around now is when the life someone has lived thus far begins to show. Sometimes it is so hard to tell how old someone is and then I find out they're younger than me or whatever and it's almost shocking. Like, really? But you look so much older! And those are the folks who've had a lot harder life than me: be it illness, death in the family, more kids, divorce, more trauma of any kind. It takes its toll and it's visible by … well, I'm going to say mid-30's.

I know enough about being a "grown-up" to know that there is not a canned answer. It's not just one thing, but it's all things. And it's different for everyone. And it's different for the same person at different ages. And really, I think that of the 7 billion people on the planet, each adult would answer that question just a little bit differently.

What I want to tell her is to enjoy each day. That she shouldn't hurry through being a kid to find out what it's like to be a "grown-up". It's not worth it and it of course goes too fast once we get there. Being a "not-yet grown-up" is pretty good, too. Sure, there's rules and regulations, but there's lots of free time and play time too, if you're lucky… and of course I'm not talking about the kids who live on the street or in orphanages and in places where they have to go to work at like 6 years old. I'm talking about the kids who get to *have* their childhoods. The kids whose parents can afford it, or they live in affluent societies, or even when they don't, they are able to enjoy some of their time by playing, kicking a ball around, and being with friends and siblings.. Yep, in this 7-year olds' world, being a kid is the way to go, and hopefully she was just askin', and not really wanting to BE grown up yet. At least, not just yet. Let's give it a few years… After all, it's complicated up here.

Excerpt Three

November 2005

Breathing hard I closed my eyes, caught in the intense rapture of the heavy moment. My thighs tighten. My back arched away from the sheets. My right hand searching for something to grasp. A sensual pressure simmered to a boil between my thighs. Steadily I moved toward the edge of my desire. Skin damp, I rocked my hips against the motion of my hand. Thinking of nothing other than what the physical would bring.

Biting my bottom lip I suppressed a moan. My body cried for release, yet I pushed myself higher before I would allow myself to tumble over the edge.   Unable to hold back. Wave after wave of pleasure assaults my senses. I can't move. I fall against the bed. I was a wet noodle left to pant alone in my bed.

Slowly my body cold. I opened my eyes, salty tears glided down my checks. I chock back a sob and roll to my side, curling into a ball. Placing my chin to my knees, I tremble. I couldn't believe what I'd just done. Never in an million years would I have thought myself capable of touching myself. Yet here I was, alone, Steven deployed again.

I hated him for making me need this. I hated the government for making him leave. I hated the e-mails that never said anything, the non-existent phone calls, the sad care packages that went out, how everything that could go wrong did go wrong, the being a single parent while he was gone, the aloneness that filled me, the absence of his scent in the house, the loss of my best friend, and the grief that sat like a stone in my gut. I was most definitely pissed at the world.

I hated all the fears that him being gone brought. The fear of him not being faithful, the fear of him not returning the same man as he left, the fear of him not wanting me when he returned, the fear of me not wanting him at all. I was drowning in my hates and fears.

In the next moment of self-indulged pity the bedroom door flew open. I screeched and grabbed the bed cover. Blonde hair ran toward me, my daughter Amelia launched herself on to the bed.

"Mom, I had a bad dream. Can I lay with you for a little while? The monsters keep licking my toes!" she said in a rush.

I didn't say a word, desperately tucking the bed cover tightly all around myself. Oh dear god...this is what I get for not locking the door.

I could see Amelia's suspicious gaze lock on me. My body heated and not in a good way. I averted my eyes afraid somehow she would know what I was just doing. I felt like a girl who just lost her virginity on the bathroom floor. I locked eyes with Amelia, trying desperately to pull off my best, "I'm the boss" look, "so you better mind your mouth". Amelia was getting too big for her britches and wondered too much about what went on in a big person's room.

"Why are the monsters licking your toes," I asked, "did you forget to take a bath before bed again?" The monsters were a new occurrence in the house that I had only been informed of a few weeks after Steven deployed.

"No, mom, I took my bath. They said I tasted sweet as honey. Do you think I'm sweet as honey mom?" Amelia tried to pull the bed cover down and climb in next to me. It was a no go. She was met with strong opposition.

"I don't think so, little one. You get your butt back in bed and kick those monsters butts." I said using my best mom tone.

"But, mom, I like your bed better," she whined.

"No, if you have a problem you face it head on. That's what daddy would say." I leaned in close to her ear, "I think he would love to hear how you kicked those monsters butts the next time he calls. So you better get to it."

Reluctantly Amelia climbed off my bed. "Okay, mom, I'll go take control of the situation. You go back to making your noise."

And just like that Amelia was gone back to her room. My mouth fell open almost with a thud. I couldn't believe it. I could have died of laughter and embarrassment all at the same time. I closed my eyes. My whole body blushed, but I'll be damned if that kid did make me smile. The day didn't seem so bad after that and I didn't feel so ashamed about what I had done.

Author's Note:

As you can guess dealing with deployments has pushed me to do things I would much rather not. But that's life; you deal with it and move on. And thank heavens for kids. They seem to make it all laughable.

Excerpt Four

March 2012

People with kids are everywhere... all over. I see people - women, specifically - who have kids and sometimes feel wistful about that. I never regret the abortion I had during my senior year of college. I was 21. I know I would not have been a good mother and even in retrospect knowing what I now know, so far not being able to have kids, I still would not have changed that decision.

Although, I went to a special eastern healer in my late 20's and he helped me find her name: it was Lily. That was a surprise. I personally have never been one of those flowery-loving women. I definitely did not pick that name on purpose.

And a few years before that my friend had a daughter who would have been almost to the month the same age as my aborted daughter's spirit. Malia and I got along so awesomely. She was like my special little gal. She was 5 when we met and I was in love instantly. We got along like peas and carrots. (I♥ Forrest Gump.) Malia and I got to have special outings to give her single mom a break and to give me my fix of a cute kid.

Anyways, I definitely feel wistful about seeing other people with kids. I know I got married late in life (35), but still. We tried to get pregnant to no avail, but not interested enough to pay oodles of $$ for this... with 7 BILLION people on the planet and counting I just didn't think it made sense.

And being adopted myself, I figured I could always adopt. We could always adopt.

Last year at a routine checkup after some weird things I found out I was pregnant... just that routine pee test. WHAT A SURPRISE!!! I was like, omg. Oh my fuck, really. I was like, oh my hell! How is that possible? Yet, it would explain so many of the physical conditions that I was ignoring.

Ignoring because of the FIRST time we tried to get pregnant and I was apparently so certain I WAS pregnant that I was inventing symptoms and then turned out to not be pregnant. What a drag, and a little embarrassing cuz I told a few people. Oh well.

I always thought that was strange, to say, 'oh we're pregnant,' or, 'oh we've conceived'… like, it's ok to say it that way but not okay to say 'oh we fucked during a rain storm on vacation.' Why is that? I always thought that was odd, since our vacationing friends told us their son was conceived during 'that big thunder storm we had last year.' Ugh. Really? Way too much information for me. I was also young, but still.

So now in my 40's, well on my way to almost infertile, it turns out that after the surprise pregnancy last year and subsequent miscarriage I feel… I feel empty a little bit. And not on purpose. I love my life. I have a great supportive husband who will do almost whatever he can to please me. We are planning a big 3-5 month trip to Europe, cuz, well, we HAD to sell the house ☹ short sale. And we have no kids. And my job contract is up in July. So what is keeping us here? Nothing is tethering us here. So we are going to take some of his inheritance and GO. And the thought is exhilarating! Really! I'm stoked. Excited. It will give me something to DO with my time – now that I finished grad school I can't believe how much free time I feel like I have. That's a whole nother story I suppose, for another time…

But 'just working' allows so much free time… free time to be wistful when I see active moms with their kids: 'that'd be me' I think… or less-than moms, surely doing the best they can – no judgment - but I definitely find myself thinking 'wow, even THAT lady had kids.'

It's not 'fair'. I whine in my head. I think of Lily. I think of last years' miscarriage. I think about all the unwanted kids everywhere, and all the 'jokes' people make about 'I've got an extra kid if you want one.' Like, really? That's great for your kids' self-esteem! And I'm thinking, yea, I'd take your kid off your hands... but since they're 'joking' I just chuckle along with them... not so funny inside.

And my favorite... when some people ask 'why DON'T I have kids?' if they find out I'm married. Well, gawd damn, just conversation but still!

Like, 'do you have kids?' is a fair enough question. It seems so logical when people meet.

What's your name?

What do you do?

Oh, you're married? Do you have kids?

People think it's like asking 'what's your favorite food?'... harmless enough.

So, it IS harmless enough.

But today I'm ranting.

And that's what journals are for, right?

I certainly wouldn't want to say this OUT LOUD to someone who is merely trying to make conversation... at any rate.

Excerpt Five

04.19.1999

Dear god I've died and gone to hell. Well me and Tessa that is because I'm sure Jaime isn't anywhere near hell after last night.

Man, I could pee myself just thinking about what happened. This spring break is turning out to be crazy.

Who would've thought a guy could have that much sex. Wait, let me rephrase that, what guy wouldn't have that much sex.

Oh no, I'm going to piddle my pants.

The way Tessa laid there at the foot of my cheap Motel Six queen size bed, on the floor trying to sleep, her face blank or almost blank, I should say. I felt bad she was on the floor. But would you really want to be in a bed with your best friends making out? She opted for the floor.

Tessa could sleep anywhere, anytime of day, and she was out. Man, I hate her for that. If I could wish for a super power it would so be that!

Back to last night. As me and Joe made out under the covers, I peeked out every now and then to make sure we weren't too loud, it was the least I could do. But each time I peeked at Tessa her slick brows were pulled tighter into a scowl. OOW, I thought. I'm in trouble. Tessa was so not sleeping. Thing was, I didn't think it was because of me. Man, I'm certain it wasn't. I peeked over at Jaime and so did Joe.

Joe was funny. We met last night. He was super cute. The kind of cute that makes you want to pinch his cheeks. We were trying to mess around, but Jaime and I'll say Mr. X (because I can't remember the poor guy's name) were having sex in the other queen bed next to us. They were loud and having angry sex. Joe couldn't concentrate on me because they were so loud. Mr. X was his good friend. I was a little bummed, but seeing Jaime and Mr. X getting it on was entertaining enough! I mean, you know that's what it looks like to have sex, but watching your friend brings it to a whole other level!

Anyhow, Joe and I popped our heads back under the covers and tried desperately not to laugh. Jaime was riding Mr. X "bronco style."

Man, Jaime didn't even try and stay covered up with a sheet or anything. I'm in good shape and all, but everything stays covered at all times. Not Jaime. She lets it all hang out. Maybe that's why guys liked her. She was confident, I'll give her that.

But seriously, there were three other people in the room.

Once Joe and I got it together, we peeked out again. Tessa now had the pillow pulled over her head working to block out the sounds of Jaime moaning. I could tell by Tessa's body language she was going to pop her top any minute. I didn't make a sound. I didn't move. I thought maybe she would forget I was there making out with a guy I just met.

Jaime started talking to Mr. X. telling him not yet. Poor guy. I didn't find out until later that she never let the poor guy get his rocks off. All that work, because from the looks of it, it was work, and no pay off. Jaime was evil.

That's when it happened. Tessa shot up like a spring, blonde hair flying everywhere, hurled her pillow at Jaime and yelled, "Come on! Shut the FUCK up and get it over with already." She stood up, walked over to my side of the bed and told me to scoot the fuck over. She laid down and stole my pillow. Joe and I looked at each other and broke out laughing so hard we both cried.

I'll always remember the look on Tessa's face, it was priceless. Disgust, irritation, and exhaustion. But you want to know what?

Jaime didn't even hesitate. She just went on riding Mr. X. I think she had bigger balls then Mr. X!

Author's Note:

This was the first road trip I ever took without my parents. I was eighteen and had two of my best friends at the time with me. We drove to Palm Springs and got a room. We spent three days there. They were three days I'll never forget. Our goal was 29 Palms, the Marine Base forty miles away. Military men were beautiful to us. Especially in their Camies. One day after we got home Joe called me and said Mr. X and he got into an accident, totaling Mr. X's truck after leaving the hotel room. They hadn't been drinking. Both Joe and Mr. X left the room around 4:00 a.m. with no sleep. They had to work. On the way home Mr. X fell asleep and crashed into a telephone poll. It was right then I knew partying and sleeping around was not for me. Not when shit like that happened. I never heard from Joe again.

Excerpt Six

10.21.1989

I can't believe what I just finished doing. I lost my virginity just now, at about 1:00 a.m. this very evening. You wanna know why? It's because I'm trippin' out on pot. I'm sooo baked right now − it's 1:30 exactly. This is the best trip I've had being stoned in my life, even better than with Brian, or at Tyler's (my first time). We laughed so hard over everything. April was being really wild, saying "We were just here − I just saw that highway sign twice in a row. I swear we already drove past it!" Y'know, like how things blur around because your eyes circle an object or they don't focus right so you think you see something twice if you're driving past it. But it was just so cool. I loved it!

Shawn was making me feel so good − the way he rubbed me in the back seat of Jason's car. Then Jason dropped off both of us in front of my house and we decided to go into the Erickson's yard (my neighbors). We were both so horny that we had to. We were rubbing each other and Shawn was hard. At first, we agreed not to, 'cause he tried, but I was afraid. Then he said, "Come on, Sarah," and I asked him if he would pull out and he said yeah. So he tried. It hurt pretty bad. It was bigger than the two fingers he'd been banging me with. We keep trying to push it in further, but it hurt, so he pulled it out when I said it hurt too bad. It hurt, but still felt good on the inside. I didn't have an orgasm. I wanted one so bad. I tried so hard. He did, as soon as he pulled out and I jacked him off.

I can't believe how stoned I was and am right now! April described being high so good. She said she was dreaming everything − it would fade and float in and out of her mind − continuously dreaming all kinds of different dreams. It was cool.

The biggest trip was going under an overpass. I thought we were going to crash into its shadow. And when Jason moved his hands over the steering wheel to screw with us, just hovering over the wheel with his hands and acting like he was actually gripping the wheel – it looked like he was turning the opposite way we were supposed to be going. Each time he'd do that us April would scream. It was really wild.

April also kept saying how she'd say things she was thinking, but didn't want to say out loud. I related to that easily. My eyes hurt because they were dry and burning. I love pot. I just had to say that because I do. I really love the pleasure it gives me. I think I love Shawn too. I wish I did for sure though. I shouldn't have fucked him, but I just had to have the pleasure at that time, so I did. Shawn is so gorgeous – I told him that. Oh well, he is! Diary – don't forget to remind me to tell you about Friday night too, about going to the Hansen's house, the train trestle, the fight between Ron and Mark at McDonald's and everything. Bye!

10.22.1989

My God! I've changed so much from last night. I'm sober now of course, and thinking back on everything makes me a little crazy. I can't believe how baked we all were.

I hope Shawn calls me – he better, at least tonight (it's only 4pm, so he has a little while yet). It's so weird looking at my handwriting and seeing how I was just babbling about everything. It's weird to think I'm not a virgin anymore. I almost want to cry because I wanted it to be so sexy and gentle. And look how it happened – in Erickson's front yard in the grass and dirt and wetness – when we were so baked out of our minds that we were so horny, we <u>had</u> to do it. I mean that, too. There's no way I could've said no – the feeling was so intense and so addicting, I couldn't stop. I had to feel him in me. It really didn't feel bad, it just stretched so much that it hurt the opening a lot!

I can't believe myself. I'm trying to tell myself that I love Shawn, but how could I? I just said, "So does this mean we are going out now?" as we were about to fuck, and he said, "Yeah." So we'd been going out for approximately one minute before we went all the way. I am a big slut. I hate the way I get so damned horny. I swear, my reputation is shit. I asked Shawn not to tell anyone, and he said he wouldn't, so maybe I shouldn't worry. The problem is me. I don't know if I can keep this inside. I keep thinking I want to tell Jennifer, since she told me about her and Micky, but I can't let anyone know, yet.

I just have to find out how I can get on the pill. I'm worried about that a lot! Even if he gets some rubbers or whatever, I still need to be on the pill, just in case. Because I know it will happen again – I just can't control my hormones with him – he makes me feel so wonderful. As long as I'm on the pill, though, maybe I shouldn't worry. I just want him to love me, that's all. I hope this incident doesn't change things between us. I don't want "us" to change. Shawn is great.

Now, about Friday night, that was one of the best nights ever! It was Nikki and Heather's birthday party. Becky and Lori put it on at Hansen's house because they were babysitting their house while they were out of town. It really was a blast. We decorated it with balloons and crepe paper, and had jungle juice made with rum, apples, bananas, pineapple, fruit punch, and Hi-C punch. It tasted alright as long as you diluted it with more punch or some lemonade before you drank it. Otherwise, the rum was way too strong. It would have been with any hard liquor though.

So anyway, Shawn showed up a little later while we played quarters, so I went outside to meet him. We just talked and smoked a couple cigarettes. It was cool though. We laughed and joked around a lot. Then we went for a walk around the college.

By the way, before we went on our walk, one of the things we were laughing about was Donna Larson. She was wasted big time. She had been passed out when we first went out on the back patio, so I helped her up and she fell right back down on the grass. After about ten seconds she let out a laugh and I helped her up again to sit on the cement steps. Then she just bent over and started puking. So we got her some water and helped her a little more. Then Shawn and I went on our walk.

We talked about how he hated cats and I loved them, and how he liked dogs, etc. – nothing big. When we got back to the house, the people in the front yard told us that Mrs. Bryce was inside, so we took off running again – back toward the college. We sat down on the hill for about five minutes, and then decided to go back to get my jacket, pillow, blanket, and clothes. We went in through the kitchen/sliding glass door. There was no way we could've got around Mrs. Bryce. Actually, Shawn was outside helping Donna and came in later. Erica and Katie went in with me. So I helped pick up about five popped balloons then got my stuff and left.

We then decided to all go to McDonald's, then out to the train trestle by Meridian. When we got there, the train was just coming, so we missed it by a mere five minutes. Me and Shawn were disappointed. So we left as soon as the train was passed, giving us about ten minutes of being at the trestle in all. We went back to McDonald's then. That's where the fight happened between Ron and Mark.

Everyone was just inside eating and talking about how they wanted to see a fight. It was pretty ironic. After everyone was pretty much done eating, we went outside and Mark and Ron were already pushing each other around. I guess it started when Ron said something about Mark's G.E.D. (something about not graduating on time), but I'm not sure. So everyone started coming out to see and the Mexicans from 7-Eleven all came across the street to watch. Ray Garcia threw two punches right at Mark's face and hit him perfectly. He got black and blue marks instantly, right next to his right eye. Mark went down with each punch (he was on the ground). Then Ron started in, calling him "Pretty Boy" and other things. Ray just kind of kept back and asked Mark if he wanted him or Ron.

Pretty soon, Mark knew he was beat and someone kind of led him to the car as he tried to get in really quick. Ray threw a couple more punches as he was getting in the car, almost hitting Mike Smith's girlfriend. She was all yelling for him to knock it off as she rolled up the window and locked the door. It was pretty funny. After the fight, I felt really bad for Mark's girlfriend. Oh well.

I forgot to say that the whole time, Shawn was right beside me with his fingers touching my neck. I loved it. That feels so good to me, kind of tickling, but giving me pleasure. Anyway, so we left with Erica and Katie, congratulated Ron when we met at the Catholic church parking lot, and went to take Shawn home. We sat in the back of Katie's truck and he had his arm around my waist, kind of squeezing my side, which I also just <u>love</u>. When we got to his house, we gave each other a quick kiss goodbye and I got in front all happy.

Then we went to Rich Merona's house to see if we could stay the night, but him and Erica got in a fight and broke up, so that was the last of those plans. There was some bitch on the couch that Rich was seeing then, and he was still seeing Erica. Oh well. So we went back to Hansen's. Luckily Mrs. Bryce was gone and people were allowed to sleep there still. So we ended up staying the night at Hansen's anyway. I went to bed pretty early too. Hurray. So that was a pretty rad night.

And so was last night, driving around tripping out with Shawn!! It was awesome. I love being that totally baked. It's a ride, let me tell you. It's great. Sorry my writing is so sloppy, I'm just getting lazy because I've written so much already and I just want to make sure I remember to tell about everything. I just remembered: when we were driving around Lakeside, I said, "I wish I had some speed." And Jason said, "You do – sitting right next to you." – meaning Shawn since that's his last name of course. We all laughed so hard over that – and boy did I ever prove them right. I did have some Speed later on that night! The funniest thing was when we were going to go to McDonald's and Jason started turning into the parking lot where there wasn't an opening – he drove up a curb. We just kind of sat there like it was nothing. Then, ten seconds later, all of us in the car started laughing our asses off all at the same time – it was the biggest trip because all of us reacted at the same very slow rate, reacting five minutes later! It was the funniest! I love Shawn and I love getting baked!

10.23.1989 10 p.m.

Everything's just wonderful with Shawn. I really think I'm going to fall in love with him fast. He's so mature and fun and everything. Tonight he came over and we did our homework together. We both had quite a bit. When we were through, I just made us a couple of sandwiches and we had some chips to eat as we watched TV. The whole time, we were just laughing at the TV shows and tickling each other a little (God I love that!), and he'd caress my hand and rub my side with his fingers. I loved it! Then I took him home and I gave him a kiss goodbye.

I forgot to say – this is so weird! Remember how me and Ron were playing the Ouija board on Friday night at the trestle? It was only for a couple of minutes, but I still can't believe what it said –

and it was true, at least some of it. Ron asked it who I would fuck next, and it spelled out S-H-A-W-N-S-P-E-E-D. Then he asked, "in how many days?" and it said 1-2-4-2. So, I'll have to figure out if that's about how many minutes it was from the time at the trestle to the time we really did "fuck" like it said. I know that we were at the trestle at about 11pm Friday night, then at Erickson's at 12:30 - 1:15am or so Saturday night. I'll have to see how many minutes that adds up to and I'll tell you if it comes out close! Scary!

10.29.1989 5 p.m.

Well, it's been a while since I've written and quite a bit has happened. April found out what we did the day after. I guess Shawn told Jason, and Jason told April ("because they tell each other everything"). Shawn went into pretty heavy detail, from what I can see. He told them where (how embarrassing!) and that I was on top. Oh well, April was super cool about it! She didn't make me feel like I was cheap or anything – she supported me really well, telling me little things about her and Jason, so I was grateful that she was neat about it.

It is Sunday afternoon. We've been going out for a week now, and we've already done it a whole bunch of times, but at least I can still count them. The second time was on Amber's birthday. My parents went to grandma's house and we stayed at the house – this is Friday at about 7:30pm. We did it on my bed. On my sheets there are places where you can see spots of blood and cum, like wet stains. It hurt pretty bad, but it also felt good. Then, we went and parked my car down on Meadowlark Road, pretty far down on the dirt road. (This was after our football game, still Friday – it had been "sleeting" (rain/snow) and it was pretty cold.) I just left the car on and we had the heat and radio on – we listened to U2's album October. It was perfect. That time, we did it probably four or five times, resting in between each. Plus, he ate me out and I gave him head. I'm going to consider this as being my first time being eaten out since I can't even remember if Lucas Wall did that time we scammed at Chris'. I was too fucked up I guess – I seriously don't remember if he did or not. Enough of that bullshit that I hate to think about.

When Shawn ate me out, it felt pretty good. He knows his "techniques" well. He made me quiver a little. The thing I loved the most is when he called out my name when we were fucking. That itself made me feel really great. He'd say "Yes, come on, come on, yes, Sarah." And be rubbing my back and legs. I was on top the whole time in the car. I forgot to say that on my bed, we tried it doggie style. I didn't know it would work that way – I always thought they put their dick in your butthole, but luckily I was wrong. It felt about the same and hurt about as much, but he had more control.

Just last night was the best (Saturday). We went over to Brad's dad's house – and we both got to stay the night. We slept in this very <u>cold</u> back bedroom, so we stayed very close the whole night (body heat!). We slept on the floor on a sleeping bag and under just a few covers. We did it doggie style, with me on top, with him on top, and we tried it sideways, but it was too difficult. I was really stoned – Joel had some "red hair," which might have been better than skunk, 'cause I was baked off two hits. I quit after that. Imagine, only two hits. I was a little drunk before we did that, so I felt just perfect. I'd had a couple wine coolers and a couple of beers with a few Marlboros. I felt great.

At first, there were quite a few people there: me, Shawn, Jennifer, Brad, Joel, Stephanie Perkins, Jen P., Jared, Daniel M., Micky, Brian Sutton, and possibly one or two more people. We watched Saturday Night Live. Then I called home, said I was staying the night at Jennifer's and Shawn called home and said "A bunch of guys are staying at Brad's, and they want me to stay." So he stayed.

When we went into the bedroom at about one, we just "fucked around" – literally. I was so stoned that I couldn't relax, and it hurt super bad, so Shawn told me to go out and get some Vaseline. I did! I didn't have anything on but a blanket around me. Joel saw and I heard them talking about it this morning when I was laying there awake. He was just saying that I didn't have anything on and I was just walking around the house. I only went to the bathroom and back. Oh well. I just have to say – when Shawn and I are "in the process," he looks so good – his facial expressions turn me on big time, because I can see how good I make him feel. And when he looks at my chest, I just seem to get turned on by his stare. Oh, I love it! At Brad's was the closest I've gotten to orgasm, but it never did come. Every time, he came before I did so he had to pull out. Next time, though!! He kept asking if I'd came yet, and I kept saying "Keep going, I will." But it just took me too long.

I think he likes me as much as I like him. I had the guts to ask him last night because of the pot, and he said he liked me a whole bunch – Great, huh!? He also said he's going to take me up skiing lots this winter. Cool, eh?! I can't wait for him to teach me. I'm so glad we've been doing so much together lately. I've been with him every day after school, doing homework, watching TV, etc. So my life is basically wonderful. Hope it lasts forever! Oh, I almost forgot! – Me and Jennifer went out looking for birth control yesterday, but most places were closed. We're going after school tomorrow to see if we can find any at Northwest Clinic or something like that. Hopefully, 'cause it's been so risky this whole week. I want to keep doing this with Shawn, but we have to have birth control, or it won't work at all.

Author's note:

This was written when I was 16 years old and a junior in high school. You might be surprised from reading this, since I sound like such a complete moron in this journal entry(!), that I got almost straight A's and was in advanced placement classes in school. I am now 39 years old. Wow, it's amazing how naïve I was! And so immature. Haha It's amazing how much I've changed from then. Thank God I didn't turn out to be a raging alcoholic or addict! I was such an idiot and so impulsive. But it was a really fun time in my life.

Shawn and I lost our virginity to each other, and even though it wasn't a well-thought-out decision for either of us, I am extremely grateful to have lost my virginity to such a great guy, and to a guy who stuck around. I also feel lucky that he came into my life at the time he did so that I didn't become more promiscuous in my quest to find love and acceptance from boys. I learned a lot about my sexuality through him and am glad that I had someone to experiment with at such a young age! We ended up dating until I left for college, so about two years. I will always consider Shawn to be my first love.

In my teens and late 20's, I was a regular binge drinker. I no longer drink more than once or twice a year because of the poor decision-making skills I had when I drank every weekend, even though I was sober during the week and fairly successful by most standards. I might smoke pot once a year or so too, but I can say that my experiences with pot are nothing like those early experiences of "tripping out on pot." That actually makes me laugh to read that! I guess pot must have felt very foreign because I hadn't figured out how much to smoke without totally losing my mind, and hadn't figured out how much I would lose control over myself when I'd be drunk and then smoke pot afterward.

I feel very lucky that I never had anything terrible happen to me because of my lack of control at that time in my life, although there were plenty of really embarrassing incidents that wouldn't have happened if I had been sober. I really just wanted my peers to like me, and hadn't been taught the skill of saying "No" in a nice way. Plus it was fun and rebellious . . . I didn't have much self-confidence other than with getting good grades, and drinking alcohol was my way to overcome shyness. Unfortunately it had the side-effect of knocking down all my inhibitions too, and I became reckless. I hope by sharing this that people will better understand the mind of a teenage girl who is searching for acceptance through sex and substance use.

Excerpt Seven

4.15.1998 7:30 a.m.

"This isn't happening! It simply can't be happening!" A few minutes from now I'm going to San Diego's Children Hospital. I'm numb all over and I can't stop thinking about how they're going to cut open Trevor's head.

He could die today and no one seems to give a shit. I can't stop shaking and I keep fighting back tears. It's really pissing me off. This sucks big time. At seventeen I shouldn't have to deal with something this huge. Eighteen-year-olds shouldn't have cysts the size of an orange growing in their head. Wow, I'm really freaking out.

Not to mention, I don't know what to wear. I put something on and rip it off. I want to look good for Trevor. It could be the last time he sees me. Oh My God, I think I'm going to be sick.

Okay, calm the fuck down. Everything will be fine.

I have to leave soon. Mom is taking me to school, but only to drop me off so Trevor and his mom can pick me up and take me with them to the hospital. Trevor's mom scares the shit out of me. All pale, white blond hair, wide mouth and those big teeth. How am I going to make it through five hours of surgery with this crazy lady? She's always asking me shit I don't understand, like she's trying to see how smart I am. Just because she and Trevor are super smart...but crazy...she looks at me like an alien. I'm smart, don't get me wrong, but not like them. I'm a common sense kind of smart. I think sometimes I look at them like they're the aliens. Anyways, I'm getting off track.

Mom is downstairs waiting. I don't want to see her. She's already worried about me. Afraid if something happens to Trevor

I'll freak out. Hell-to-the-yes, I'm going to freak out. Trevor's my first love, my first everything. I'd do anything for him. He fills me with life. Oh, man...I really think I'm going to be sick. I have to leave, but I'm taking my journal with me. I won't make it through the day if I can't write down everything.

11:03 a.m.

Finally I can write. Trevor has been in surgery for two hours now. And I've managed to hide from Ms. Smith successfully. I'm sitting under a nice shade tree by the hospital. The sun is out and it feels good on my skin popping through the leaves and branches. Sigh...I can't believe what Ms. Smith said. Trevor is never going to believe this when I tell him. Wait, no, I better not, it's just one more thing to make him want to move out sooner. I don't want to think about it anymore.

Okay, let me get you up to speed on the last three and a half hours of my life. I'll start where I left off. Then you'll understand why I'm hiding.

When I walked down stairs to leave this morning I found my mom sitting at the dining table staring blankly at the wall with a cup of coffee in her hand. All she needed was a cigarette and it would have been just like a movie.

That's probably why I felt so disconnected, it was too much like a movie.

I can see it now. A first time lover is stricken with an illness. An illness the doctors couldn't cure and a dangerous surgery is the light at the end of a very dark tunnel. Man!

I told mom I was ready and grabbed my backpack.

She looked like crap. I knew this was going to happen. Tears stung my eyes. I hated her. I was trying to be brave. And she was making it so hard sitting there looking all broken hearted. Parents!

She told me I could call if I wanted to leave. She would come get me. I nodded. And told her I love him. And that I had to be there. Anguish filled me. Trevor was so young. Why was this happening?

We walked out of the house not saying another word. Mom dropped me off at the back of the high school where I waited for Trevor and his mom.

Ten minutes passed before they came driving up the road. I still can't believe Trevor's mom made his brother and sister go to school. It didn't seem fair.

The air grew heavy and pushed down. I wanted to crumple to the sidewalk.

I watched Trevor climb out of the Jeep to allow his brother and sister out from the back. He said good-bye and tried to act as if it was just another day.

Trevor's brother and sister walked on to the school campus. They didn't look back.

Can you believe that! Trevor's family dynamic is so weird. Sorry got off track again.

The drive to Children's Hospital was spent in silence bouncing down the freeway. Trevor had a death grip on my hand and pulled me into his side. Apprehension oozed from his pores. He looked deathly white. His freckles stood out on his face and said, "Here we are!"

I wanted to bury my face in his chest and tell him how much I loved him and how happy I was to have him in my life. But I couldn't, not with his mother sitting in the front watching us from the rearview mirror.

Please. For Christ's sake. I wasn't going to make out with him right there in the back seat. Man, I wanted to stick my tongue out at her so bad.

I'd looked out the window of the Jeep and stared blindly at all that passed until I saw the hospital standing on the hillside of the 805 freeway. My stomach knotted again.

I managed to hold it all together, that is until we met with the doctor.

The consultation room was small and compact. There were no windows on any of the four barren walls which constructed the room. I sat in one of the three worn out looking chairs the doctor presented to us after entering the room. The silence was unsettling. The room frightened me and I squeezed Trevor's arm, fighting back a wave of tears.

How could I possibly be strong for him when my gut rolled like a bowling ball down a lane! I hated hospitals more than anything in the world. It was the grim reaper's welcomed haven.

I sucked in a deep breath and pushed my fears aside as best I could. I listened to the doctor as he spoke to Trevor and his mother about how the operation would go. The doctor made the whole procedure sound so easy.

I threw up in my mouth a little.

The thought of someone poking around Trevor's brain was very disturbing. This was my best friend and here I sat in a hospital consultation room praying he wouldn't die.

Afraid of what was coming shortly I noted the lack of smell in the room. Hospitals reeked of death, yet here I smelled nothing. No odor at all. My chest tightened. At least in the part of the hospital that dripped with death you knew what it held, but here there was nothing. It was a void. I shivered.

Before I realized it, the doctor, Mrs. Smith, Trevor and myself stood in a long carpeted corridor that would take Trevor to be prepped for surgery. The walls were coated in a dark mauve making it feel bleak and closed in.

Trevor pulled me into his arms. He told me he loved me with all his heart and that the last two years we had been together was his heaven. He told me thank you for loving him.

What the hell do you say to that? I fell apart.

I tried to pull away, to upset to talk. Yet, Trevor wouldn't let me go, he only gripped me harder. He held me in silence for several moments. He kissed me with full lips, passionately, then let me go. He set me on fire with that kiss. Scorching my soul. I would be dead without him.

I heard Trevor talking to his mom, but all I thought about was the kiss and how there was no smell in the corridor, just as in the consultation room. Two metal stainless steel doors swung open at the end of the long hall Trevor and his doctor passed through. I stood frozen. Trevor's tall lean body was rigid as if preparing for battle.

I finally cracked. Tears washed over my face. Trevor smiled then turned away. The steel doors closed like the shutting of a book. Trevor was gone and I felt completely alone even with Mrs. Smith beside me. My knees buckled and I sank to the ground, there in the middle of the corridor. I couldn't breathe. I started seeing spots. I was going to pass out.

To my surprise a skinny hand yanked me to my feet.

"Don't you cry in front of me you little slut." Trevor's mom said to me hatefully, "You've no idea what it feels like to have some stupid girl steal my son's affection."

I so was shocked. You could have knocked me over with a poke of a finger. The bitch called me a slut, when her son was the first person I ever slept with. I was falling apart and I had to deal with her. I should've known the crazy would come out.

I yanked my arm free and looked her square in the eye.

"What's wrong with you?" I shouted, managing to push all thought of Trevor to the back of my mind. It was on! Ms. Smith was going down.

"You," she croaked at me. I was on fire. I felt the flames dancing on the top of my head. I had never done anything to her. Trevor always told me she was crazy, now I knew why he always said that.

"Your son is back there..." I pointed to the large stainless still door. "Back there about to have his skull opened to try and relive some of the pressure on his brain and here you stand in the middle of a hallway saying mean things to his girlfriend."

Ms. Smith's light blue eyes narrowed. I didn't even know if she was listening. I didn't pretend to know what was going on in her head.

I walked away and left her in the middle of the hallway alone.

Please God, be with Trevor. Protect him. Help him through this surgery. Find a way to stop his pain.

***

Oh man! I'm crying again. Who knew you could cry this much in one day. I feel like a faucet, only I can't shut off. Is that not some crazy, for you? I don't think I can go back in there and face that lady. I just want to be sad. I have to be ready, just in-case something goes wrong.

My stomach is talking to me, yet I have no appetite. I've been shaky for the last hour, though I'm not sure if it is from lack of food or because this is a terrible day.

8:43 p.m.

I made it. And so did Trevor. I'm so tired. I can hardly keep my eyes open. I don't think I could do this again. It is too emotional a thing. Having someone you love in pain. Here is the skinny on the rest on the rest of the day.

I finally caved and went to get something to eat. All the food looked awesome in the cafeteria hospital. I didn't know what to get. I settled on a bowl of fruit and a Dr. Pepper. But, right when I got to the cashier I heard the speaker sound overhead. Paging Mrs. Smith. Shit. Trevor! I left my food and took off to the east wing of the hospital in a sprint. I kept my eyes peeled for Mrs. Smith. It was really sad; hiding from the one person I should be supporting. I felt bad, but not that bad.

Battling with myself as I ran I spotted Mrs. Smith at the nurse's desk, her eyes were red puffy and blood shot. She'd been crying. A huge wave of guilt hit me hard almost toppling me over. She spotted me as I slid to a halt. She froze.

Together we walked to the recovery side of Children's Hospital. I asked for Trevor Smith at another nurse station. One of the nurses pointed to the hall off to the right and there was Trevor pasty white and not moving. I started shaking bad. He looked terrible. Bandages over his head and side of his face. Hot tears rushed down my cheeks again. My baby. My Trevor. Everything inside me screamed for him. I had to touch him. Had to know he was still there. I rushed to the side of the gory as the nurses wheeled him into what was going to be his room.

I almost fainted, but held it together.

Trevor was trying to talk. Half drugged he managed to call for me. Me! Over and over. He hadn't stopped until I took hold of his hand.

"I'm right here. Right beside you. Don't worry I'm here." I told him. I choke back a sob. He was okay. He made it. It was over.

Rapidly, Trevor had been taken by the drugs to a dead zone. He was so out of it. Only his chest rose and fell unaware of all the happenings that were taking place around him.

As the nurses buzzed about his room I only saw him. I could breathe for the first time all day. The tightness in my chest eased. I sank to the side of his bed and stared at him. Watched him breathe. I made it, he made it, but I didn't think Mrs. Smith made it. I stole a glance at her and she looked like shit. But she hadn't gotten close to us. And then it hit me. Trevor had asked for me, not her. For her no matter what she'd lost her son. A tear fell for her.

Author's Note:

This was the second time Trevor had been to surgery. We started dating not too long after the first surgery. I hadn't known there was anything wrong with him. It was very hard to handle because I was so young. We stayed together for another year, but things changed. We grew apart as first time loves so often do. And his mom always hated me. That was until he started dating someone else she hated more than me. Then she was nice after that. When she saw me every now and again, she would say that me and Trevor just needed to work it out...

9.12.1999

I glared at the ring on my finger. Hate burning inside of me. Tears washing my cheeks. I yanked the ring off and chucked it at the bathroom wall. It tinked off the tile and slid to a new home with the shattered pieces of my heart I didn't care to find.

I choked on a sob. I hated Trevor for this. For causing this to happen. I would never forgive him, of that I was sure. All the stress was just too much for my body. He wasn't supportive about any choice I tried to make. Desperate to find a way to fix the situation without taking a life and destroying two.

The restroom was an icy tomb, heavy with the scent of blood. Curled in the corner, my gaze darted to the toilet. My stomach contracted painfully. My mouth watered, my skin covered in sweat, the urge to vomit was overpowering. I wanted to look away. To crawl deep within myself and hide from the truth that was set before me, yet I couldn't. My eyes remained anchored squarely on the toilet.

The water was dark with the life blood that was mine and my baby's. Four and a half months I shared my body with this tiny little being. And I loved that little person more than the future I worked so vigorously to create in school. Now, it was gone.

I wiped my tears, grief consuming me causing my eyes to slam shut. Sorrow spilled out in all directions mixing with the icy air. I suffered in silence, not making a sound. I wanted to reach into the watery grave of my first born child and save it. I knew I couldn't. It was too late and it had come too early. No one could help me. I chewed my bottom lip until it bled.

With my head rested on my knees, shattered, broken in a way I could never be fixed, I cradled my empty slightly round belly. It seemed my body was in denial of the rapid miscarriage. I knew if the placenta didn't come out, I could slowly bleed to death. Yet, I didn't care if I died. I hated myself and my body for doing this.

Rising upon shaky legs, struggling to pull myself together. I placed my trembling hand on the toilet handle. It was cool. I took a deep breath closing all the doors to my frantic emotions. Sealed them tight. Then I did the hardest thing in my life. I flushed the toilet. And went back to work.

***

Weak and still bleeding, I drove myself home after somehow making it through my shift at work. I could've asked to go home early, but my boss would've wanted to know why. I would never tell. No one knew I was pregnant. It had been mine and Trevor's secret.

By the time I got home, dark spots blinked in and out of my vision. I made my way into the house and up the stairs to my bathroom. My stomach hurt so bad I could hardly move. Quickly I pulled my pants off and sat on the toilet. Blood ran freely. I started crying. I wanted to call Trevor and tell him what was happening. But I couldn't because I knew there would only be relief in his voice. I knew I couldn't handle that right then. He hadn't wanted this baby. Neither had I. When I had taken the pregnancy test months ago and it was positive, a thought instantly popped into my head. I don't want to have Trevor's baby. I knew that wasn't the kind of reaction someone had when they loved the person they were with. I loved Trevor, but I wasn't in love with Trevor anymore. He had changed after his brain surgery. Grew distant. Started hanging out with bad people from school. He thought he was going to die so he just didn't care anymore about anything. Not even me and the life we made together.

I shoved on my stomach. Kneading it. I had to get the placenta out or I was going to the hospital if it wasn't already too late. Crying and beating my lip I finally heard the splash I was waiting for.

I looked in the toilet. There was too much blood, but I had to be sure. I reached into the water and found what I was looking for. I lifted it up. Thank god. I threw it back in. How do you survive a death of a child? I didn't know and I wasn't sure I would. I felt stained. I would never be clean again.

Cleaned myself up after the bleeding slowed. I crawled into bed and thought about how I was going to tell Mrs. Chris I no longer had a baby to give her and her husband. How was I going to tell her I lost her baby? I cried the whole night alone.

Author's Note:

This took place one year after Trevor's brain surgery. I was now eighteen and a senior in high school. After the miscarriage, a few days later I told Trevor what had happen and told him it was over. He didn't care, even said thank you. So much for true love. We had been together for three and a half years.

Excerpt Eight

12.25.2001

I cannot sleep… It's already midnight and I have been up 2 hours rearranging my room. So much is running through my mind… God, and our relationship (ain't so good right now) my life, my future, who I am…

The other day Sherry and I were talking and she asked me if I knew who I was… I said yes… then I felt almost sure but now I'm unsure. Who am I? And do I like who I am? Well, I am Kara Marie Carson, age 14 (15 in 3 weeks), daughter of Dale and Ruth Carson – those are facts but inside, in my soul, where am I headed? What's my purpose? I know a few things about my inside – I mean I sort of understand my feelings, attitudes, moods from experience. But there's some things I don't know… like why do I hate myself so much at times? I am so hard on myself – I mean I don't usually show my self-esteem but inside and in the hidden spots I call myself loser and idiot, stupid, whatever I can think of at the moment. Why? I'm not that bad of a person … I mean I want to do good and I usually try my best to be.

I guess sometimes I feel like a hypocrite… But I know things need time – it's all in good time - I should be humble and patient and wait on the Lord to guide my path… but life becomes so monotone… I just wish I could fall head over heels in love with God and stop my longing for another's love… I mean I know God is just waiting with open arms but once again, I'm not patient.

Well, now I'm tired… just thought I'd jot down my confusion of thoughts since Sherry gave me this journal.

Well – Adios!

May 2002

Today I sat looking at myself in the mirror. I have never really thought myself attractive or pretty and I certainly do not meet up to the requirements of a model. But as I stared at my nude body reflected in the mirror, something in my head said, "Kara, you are beautiful and that is because your body is pure, unabused and unscarred." I suddenly felt like crying as I came to this realization that not just me but my body also deserves and should be saved for that special someone who would love and treat it with utmost care.

Growing up over the years I, just like any girl, have wished and dreamed of being lovingly held in a man's arms and many times I have compromised my values just to feel a few moments of pleasure, comfort and security.

It is hard to put into words what I am trying to say… I guess it is that I have always thought that any sexual activity I would ever have would affect only my mind and feelings even though my body would be the connector. But now I feel I've come to the realization that my body is precious because of its purity and only is to be touched and given to the one that I spend my life saving it for.   Like a savings account… the money poured in there is precious because of the time and patience it spent to save it and it is more precious each day because it is added to. So when it is finally used on the end result for which it was needed, it is obvious how much all the effort of saving was worth it!

Perhaps this is not a great revelation to you but I now feel much better about myself and my values, which I am determined now to uphold until I marry the man who is truly worthy. In the meantime, I will draw closer to my Lord and learn to be more like Him so that I will also be worthy of a man who saves himself for me.

09.10.2002

I promise in all my years I will never forget this day. It's still all so unreal to me. I keep thinking, "This isn't happening."

Today Daddy died. I can't believe it. He's gone forever... he won't be at my graduation, at my wedding, here for Christmas, 4th of July, Valentine's, all those holidays we celebrated together. When I found out... I didn't cry. Not for a long time. I saw a glimpse of him through the bedroom door. It only looked like he was sleeping!

Right now I am breaking down... I want to say "Finally!" but then again I want to stay under control. Dear God, help me to know what to do! What should a person do in this sort of situation? I feel like I shouldn't keep on smiling, laughing, eating and all those things we do daily. But then again, I'm still not sure if it has hit me... you know, the fact that he is really gone... forever.

I keep thinking, "Why, God?" He was the best, most humble, loving, awesome man I have ever known.... No words could ever tell how great a man he was! Oh, why can't he come back! Oh, God, it hurts.... My husband will never know... my children will never know him or what an awesome man he was.

I should stop feeling selfish and remember that he is finally in no more pain and he's in a better place... he finally got to see Jesus. The one he loved more than anything. Oh, but the memories keep flooding back, and how I am going to miss him! Daddy, I love you so much more than you could have ever known!

I know his life will never have been in vain. Every day he lived he taught me something new. I want to take these lessons and try with everything within me to be more like him.

12.25.2002

I wish you were here, with me, in my room again. I need to talk to you right now. Earlier I had nothing to say but now I know I need to talk to someone... not just an old notebook. I know I could call... I know you would listen and care and try to understand. So why don't I? Well, like I was telling you earlier, people may compliment me but I can't bring myself to believe them. I continue to be self-critical. I find all my imperfections and point them out. And I worry galore! Like tonight, I keep asking myself, "Did I share too much with him? Did I give him any wrong impressions?" I don't trust enough. I'm so afraid of sharing a part of myself and knowing that someone else knows a secret part of me.

Right now I really feel that I NEED, have to, share a secret with someone. I want to tell my sister... but will she listen? ... will she hear my cry for help? Will anyone!? I wish I could tell you... but it would probably damage you to find out that I have such major weaknesses too. I should be a strong friend who is secure and self-assured, but I'm not. I'm quite the opposite.

In so many ways I can relate to your depression and I have problems that everyone is unaware of. I wish I could feel free to talk to you. I am really going to miss you for the next few days.

  Love Kara

05.18.2004

I can't stop thinking, and I feel I need to write. I can't sleep. Why did I drink the coffee? That's what my problem is and now my hand is shaking.

Anyways, I don't know where I am at, where I stand right now. I wonder if anyone else does. We all act as normal as possible and try to ignore it, except Mom. She seems to be facing her need to find the straight path. Maybe it's just the way my generation is, or maybe it's just me, going cold. I don't like where I am at. I don't agree with what I am doing. I know I am wrong right now. I miss God, but I am hanging, just hanging. My face unmoved, unchanged. No emotions and I hate it. I'm very confused and I want to talk but they would be so ashamed. "look at that black sheep. That hanging, black sheep. So lost. Just dripping and hanging, not moving but maybe sinking.

How sad that my questions can't be answered by the one who I know loves me most because I am her flesh and a piece of her womb and nature. My questions would gouge her and wound her more than heal my painful wonderings. Why, so suddenly, do I find it so unenjoyable? Why does it feel mechanical suddenly? Why do I desire to push away and say "You filthy dog!" But I don't because I know he's not and I know I love him. I read about and heard stories about other women who felt this way at times too. I didn't understand then. Thought they must be kinda crazy. Now I understand and I am so afraid. How did it get here? Each time, the farther it goes, so does my desire, out the door... why?

I don't know that I want it back right now, but will it ever return or will I always be a robot? A bitch, a cow – mounted, conquered – but knowing, feeling that what drives him is not him, but beyond him. Or am I just hoping that? I think I have an idea why my problem is here. It's not right. Wrong time, wrong place, wrong everything. But what is, when it's supposed to be right my problem is the same?

Finally, I cry! But the damn tears are so short in supply. What if I just let it all go? Give him all of me because I love him and he is driven? I don't want to – I'm afraid to. The pressure is there, but also it is not. I could back up, but I don't know how. What would I back up into? But what is ahead? Shame? Separation? Loss? All because I am hanging, and accepting such a ridiculous position.

I want to talk but the caring arms would close when they see the double-sided sword in my heart that would stick in theirs if they listen to me. Other arms appear caring, but they've never been tested and I'm risking crazy exposure! I wish to run away or sleep. Maybe both, together, would be pleasant. No, pleasant doesn't exist. Oh, anything but hanging! I think that is all I can do so I suppose I will hang… just hang. Hang loose.

08.10.2004

Since three months ago, I have mended some things. I don't think I am hanging anymore and I thought I had overcome something that was once impossible for me. However, no one else seems to see my progress. That hurts… Oh God, that hurts so bad!

This problem used to burn in my conscience every day, every minute. It was driving me to the brink of insanity because I knew what I should do, but I didn't think I could do it. Finally, I cried out to God… seriously… I got very desperate and things just seemed to flow from there. But now, it just all seemed to flood back.

I know I should not live for other people and that it was God that changed my desires to His, but I can't seem to forgive myself. I continue thinking "It doesn't matter." I want to believe nothing matters… that it doesn't hurt but all those old hurts and all that old condemnation flooded back.

On one hand I want tomorrow to come because I think I will forget but then I don't want it to come because it's another day and I almost wish I could fall asleep and never wake. I was beginning to feel comfortable and right again because I had gotten things cleaned up. But I guess not… I am still plain rotten. I need to stop feeling sorry for myself and just forget about it all… just not care about anything… how I look …. I guess I am just vain.

Author's Note:

Wow! In these three years of journaling, I had obviously been going through a lot of changes and I was right in the midst of so much self-discovery. I was fifteen when my father died of cancer and I remember the following teenage years as being very, very difficult. I feel that these entries were important in reflecting the confusion I was facing and mostly the spiritual challenge that I was being confronted with. I was not very thorough in explaining the situations surrounding my frustrations, so this is where I will provide some background.

I was raised in a strict religion in which women were often subtly subjugated through the tight restrictions and expectations placed upon them. I was told that wearing anything besides a long skirt that passed below my knees, even when sitting, was unacceptable and sinful. Other prohibited apparel was jewelry, short-sleeved shirts, make-up, hair dye, and even trimming my hair was sacrilegious. There were also "holiness standards" that males had to follow, but when it came to the public scene (especially public school) the females stood out like sore thumbs in how drastically different they appeared to the average American girl. Of course, there were other social restrictions placed upon us young folks, such as, no television, no movies, no dating until sixteen or sometimes older, no dating without a chaperone, no touching of the opposite sex and you must maintain a certain distance from them (six inches or something), no mixed swimming, no playing on school sports teams, no attending school sports games, etc. The biggest problem was that these rules often shifted from church to church, and from the time I was a child until 19 years old, my family had attended about five different locations, and though many of the rules were the same, I had to learn the new details of each every time we went to a new church. On top of all of this, my father was a minister and on a few occasions, was the head pastor of one or two churches that we attended and I was often expected to play a leading role during services. To say the least, this put a lot of pressure on me to have the best behavior and to step up to responsibility.

Before my father died, he had started his own church and we had been running it for about two or three years before he passed away. This church was not "approved of" by the other local organized congregations for some ridiculous reasons based on the pastors being full of themselves and on a constant power trip, believing fully that every word that came from their mouths was "the Word of God!" So, if they told my dad he could not start a church, then he was going against God's will to do so, and so they had "discommunicated" our family. This had actually happened on a few occasions to not only our family, but also close friends of ours. Obviously, it was a dramatic life to be living! Interestingly enough, about a year before my dad died, he started questioning this religion we were claiming to follow and he openly vocalized his concerns even preaching that we were no better than any other religion in the town, which would have been like treason to the ears of other pastors of this same religion. He also answered some of my questions about how I could behave with boys and social situations, like watching movies and attending football games in a very different manner than previous pastors had. He began teaching my brother, sister and I that he trusted our judgment, and allowed us to watch movies at friends' houses, attend school ball games, and told me it was okay to kiss a boy or hold his hand under certain circumstances. He died within a year of these new perspectives coming into our lives.

My brother and sister both left the religion within a year or two of dad's death because they had both graduated and left home. I was living with my mom and did not feel confident enough to do so at that time. As is probably obvious from my entries, I had met a boy in high school and began "falling in love." My father had met him, but barely, considering he was quite distracted from many things while fighting cancer that last year of his life. This boy, Ricky, was a "bad boy," a wanna-be gangster, and lived in the ghetto. I wanted to be his savior and bring him to salvation, but soon, he led me down his path and I began doing things that were considered inappropriate by the standards of my religion.

After my father's death, my mom and I began attending a church that had disagreed with my father's church and would not have talked to us previous to his death, but somehow they had convinced my submissive and easily persuaded mother that she had been misguided by my father and needed to come back to the "right" church. I was certainly confused about this, but hoped that these people wanted the best for us and followed my mother to that church, which was a big mistake. I got Ricky to start attending the church with me, but he did not like the pastor much, which I discovered later he had good reason not to. The pastor became very nosy about my interactions with Ricky and I soon felt very guilty and ashamed for having made out with him on multiple occasions and allowing him to touch me underneath my clothes, although I did not share these secrets with anyone. When I wrote about my guilty conscience, it was about these "inappropriate" things that I had done with Ricky.

As I mentioned in one entry, I was confused about my feelings for Ricky. On one hand I was sometimes attracted to him, and other times repulsed because I was confused about what my boundaries were and very frustrated with the pressures from my current pastor and pressures from Ricky's expectations since I had already opened a few doors to his desires. However, I wanted to cling to him because he was a person I felt I could be honest to about my confusions and he was always there to show me love and attention. He was a bit stressful to me as a few of my future entries will reveal, because he was really quite a needy person and somewhat of a loser, a high school drop-out that couldn't land a job because he could never pass a drug-test!

These last two entries indicate the major condemnation I felt from this new pastor. Although I did not write about it, strange things were happening. When I first started attending there, he would have private meetings with me to discuss my "wayward" past, led by my father. He discussed his opinion about my father's choices, which of course he believed was righteous and in accordance with God's opinions. He even talked about my parent's sex life, which was so awkward for a sixteen-year-old girl! And he also commented on my choice of apparel, saying that my clothes were too tight and revealing and basically, I needed to get a new wardrobe. Perhaps this was accepted by my dad, but not at his church. He discussed this with my mother and we went shopping for new clothes, which we really didn't have the money to be doing, and I felt guilty about that for my mother. It was around this time that I started "mending a few things" as I wrote in my journal. What that meant was that I wasn't seeing Ricky anymore and I was trying to do what this new pastor expected of me. Then, a few weeks later, he called me into his office again, just to tell me and my mom that my wardrobe was still not satisfactory. He even went so far as to name specific outfits that I had worn that were not acceptable because they "exposed the curve of my thighs," etc. He had his wife give me a demonstration on how my shirt should fall over my breasts and not curve under them to reveal their shape or size! This was so, so devastating and shocking! I felt so humiliated and ashamed when I hadn't intended to do something wrong. I thought I had been doing things right. I almost felt molested by the way he knew exactly what clothes I had been wearing and when and how he described how they looked on me. Why had he been watching so closely!? It was then that I *wrote those last two entries describing how dirty and shameful and ugly I felt. It was already hard to go to public school wearing a long skirt and shirts that covered everything, but now I had to wear large, baggy clothes that I bought in the women's section, because the junior section was "too revealing" for my young, blossoming figure. I couldn't help that my breasts were growing larger and that I was one of the only girls in the church that actually had an ass and some thick thighs! All the other girls were either fat, or flat as a rod all around. It came from my mother's genes to have a full figure and it was so hard to hide it and be ashamed and embarrassed of it all through my high school years because of this ridiculous and perverted pastor.*

I feel these past entries and the ones to come were important in showing the journey I took to discover my spirituality and my perspectives of the world as I was heading for adulthood. Sometimes I am embarrassed about how much I talked about God in some of these entries, but I really wanted to believe in Him, although I was struggling with what kind of God He was and what kind of God I believed Him to be.

The next entries reveal a girl who was once a caged bird, but begins to seek out and demand an explanation for her questions and confusions and in doing so, she finds she must defy everything she was told to be right and wrong in order to make sense of it for herself and come to her belief about it all.

12.24.2004

It does not feel like Christmas Eve at all. I suppose that is because I base how it should feel on how it used to feel. I miss the excitement for the next morning. I miss that innocence.

Looking at my past struggle, I realize how strange it is that in one night my struggle can be eradicated. However, it seems I thought I had been delivered before but I simply turned right back around to my own vomit. How awful! But now I can see clearly all the lies I told myself and all the truths I had. I knew things were wrong and I could not fix them with a plan that I actually didn't truly like. I knew when he lied to me about such stupid things! He manipulated left and right and I allowed it! What a fool! And that right there is why I continued allowing it. I felt guilty. Guilty for allowing his first step in the first place. I kept returning to him because I was ashamed and felt that was what I deserved. So many times there was such a great wave of repulsion and disgust with him and his clinginess. Then I would force myself to think, "Oh, look how handsome he is and he needs my help," and so on, with stupid excuses.

I'm so glad I can see things clearly and I am actually handling it right. I am so glad someone, a man, took time to make me step back and uncover the truth and accept it. I knew that was what was needed all along. My imagination knew I needed the strength of a man to reassure me, aid my weaknesses. I wish I could always and forever keep in remembrance those words that saved me. Perhaps I will, for they have been running through my head for days.

Of course I have regrets… but then again, I don't. I have hurt and learned and grown. I threw pictures away but not the letters. However, I stored them away. There are countless memories and I won't delete them. For some reason, they don't hurt as I thought they would. When I talk to him on the phone the feelings are completely gone. I feel frustrated very often, but I pity him and pray for the day when he will lean on God and not me.

02.21.2005

The strangest thing happened tonight. I thought about getting drunk… I was actually wondering how I could get alcohol because I can't sleep and I want to just forget and not think about anything. I can't stand the way I am lately. My thoughts are so depressed and I really abhor it. I know better than this! But then I just don't care. It all feels empty... numb. I can't explain it any other way... just don't care. But I know this is not right but I feel too weak to know what to do.

When the tears came, I hated them. Then I see the hairs that have fallen from my head on my pillow. What is happening to me?! Sores on my mouth... ambition dying. I don't even feel excited about college next year. I have many worries which pass through my mind and I know I should not allow myself to think this way. But should not someone other than this journal know of my loneliness, hurt and fears?

I just need to stop feeling sorry for myself. It is my own fault that I don't talk and I am not the only person who has suffered.

05.24.2005

Tomorrow is the big day. I don't feel nervous or strange. It seems as if tomorrow will be just another day. But it is not because I have waited for this day since grade school. I can recall the time I figured out that 2005 would be the year I would graduate from high school and it seemed decades away! I was sure I could not wait that long for life to begin. Now I am unsure if I am even ready for tomorrow and all that comes beyond.

Today I heard a friend talking about how her dad returned home from Iraq and she was so happy to see him and give him a hug. It reminded me suddenly that Dad will not be at my graduation tomorrow. His most important hug will not be there for me. I have not thought of this since he died, but now 2½ years have passed and the first big event in my life is here, but he is not. However, awhile back when I was grieving about Dad, I realized something... I still have Mom. Oh goodness! What would I do without her and I need to appreciate her more.

09.21.2005

Today I was working on my assignment for my Bilingual-Education class and part of the requirement is to observe the neighborhood of the children we are studying. I have already driven around the trailer park on Sunday, but I wanted to go again to take some pictures and such. I noticed some things today that I have noticed and felt before, but never really voiced. As I drove around, people seemed to look at me strangely, like they knew I did not "belong" there. Now I really don't know if that is merely my assumption of what they think… it is possible they look at everyone that way. But I had the feeling that they understood I did not live there. Was it my car? I saw nice, newer cars parked around sometimes. Was it my skin color? I saw other white girls and women. Was it my dress and demeanor? I don't know, but I certainly felt excluded. Was this feeling of exclusion my own presumption and defense mechanism because of previous experiences?

It makes me think of the way I sometimes felt when I went to Ricky's house on the North side of Nampa. I got that same feeling of exclusion. Once, when Ricky and I were standing outside, Karl from school happened to drive by… he stopped and said, "What are you doing here? I never thought I would see you on the North side!" He didn't mean it rudely, but he proved that what I was feeling was the truth. I tried to deny what he said and thought to myself, "I can belong here just as well as you," but I knew within myself that wasn't true.

By that time, I had been in that neighborhood enough times to feel generally comfortable there and I think the neighbors (Ricky's) had become used to seeing me there, too. However, I don't think I was quite welcomed as a "member," but more as a "visitor." Did they understand within themselves that I was just "another uptown girl going with a backstreet boy?"

So where does all this lead to? I do believe I have a conclusive point and thought to this. I was thinking today after driving back from the trailer park about what did those people think I was thinking about them as I drove through their territory? Did they think I thought their way of life was lower than mine? Did they realize I cared about them, was interested in them… and not just on a distance level, but on a level that I would like to experience their lives? If I told them that, they would laugh in my face because I am an intelligent, "rich" white girl who, of course, would never wish such a thing?

11.26.2005

My sister talked to me the other day about my dreams. She reminded me I once had dreams. I don't believe it is so much that I have begun to forget my dreams but I have begun dismissing them because I do not believe myself important enough or worth my dreams. I mean, ME an altruistic person who gives of herself to people less fortunate? No, not me. That's for heroes and I am not a hero. My thoughts have often been resting upon radical whims, chaotic reactions that will surprise the world – or rather, my world. The reason I feel hypocritical is because I know who and what the world perceives me to be is not who I am.

I really am wild and eccentric with exotic, sensual dancer tendencies. However, I do enjoy the appearance of a timid, reserved girl who's "got it all together" because that is also somewhat of what I am. Okay, so everyone has an alter-ego but I guess what I am trying to get at is that I want to live my life and behave voluntarily!

I once explained to Ricky how the knowledge that I cannot have something or something is impossible; beyond my reach… this thought drives me crazy! I choose not to eat at McDonald's, but if I passed by it every day knowing that I had no money to eat there, that would make me crazy! Perhaps I have had choice so much in my life that I expect to have it always. I am so thankful my sister reminded me of my dreams. She has done that before, reminded me that I have a choice and I am worthy of a choice. The thing about religion is that I want to do it voluntarily. I like wearing skirts and I like my hair. I feel like a lady, respected in them. But I hate that the world may believe I do it all because of religion, because I am afraid to try something different.

I want to want God voluntarily and in some ways I feel like I have to get away from here, away from everything connected to my past so that I can come to God and religion with a new perspective. I know I cannot ever separate myself from my past and background and I don't wish to do that because it is my make-up. But now I really want to go to another country. I want to go where I can be who I am because that is who I am and not because that's what I feel I am expected to be.

I looked up the word "lonely" in the dictionary. It has all sad connotations (sad because one has no friends or company... (without companions). But I don't quite see loneliness that way. Yes, I have mourned and been sad because I felt alone but then I got over that when I realized I love my solitude! Also, I have many close companions and also surface acquaintances, which are comforting. But all my internal thoughts and feelings are mine and I like to visit them by myself very often. I share them sometimes but they could never be completely shared. I like the definition given for a lonely place... "unfrequented and remote." That's my loneliness inside. It's beautiful, quiet and serene. I can't go to another country right now, but I can wait and let God work on my head for now.

Author's Note:

It is pretty obvious that at this point I was starting to strongly question this religion I was brought up to believe in. This was a very crucial and stressful time in my life. Crucial because I knew that making the decision to leave something that I had been pressured to identify with all my life, I knew I would never turn back on that decision. I have come to understand that a characteristic of my personality and behaviors is that I make decisions sometimes quickly and sometimes through much thought, but I rarely change my mind about my decisions. I am decisive and I could feel this strongly at this time in my life. I was tired of living a lie, and claiming strong statements as directed by pastors and peers, when I really questioned those "truths," as they called them.

I remember that the day I decided to leave the church was around the first of January, the beginning of a new year. I did not record this event in my journal, but it is evident in the following passages.

01.14.2006

What am I saying? What am I feeling? I am just feeling... is that not life? Is that not what the living do and the dead do not? Is not *feeling* the gulf that separates and distinguishes life from death? Well, I lost the one that I loved... loved with my life. I saw his corpse through the doorway. He was sleeping, so it seemed. I did not crumble as I always imagined it should happen. Why? Because I had to live.

Sometimes... well, actually always... I feel lost because I don't know what part of Dad is inside of me anymore. I don't know what life is anymore and at one time I felt I knew what life was because I was sure of what Dad was... *was* – it is past tense.

I want to be a true person. Perhaps because of what morals I have been raised with or perhaps because it is a romantic notion... follow your dreams! "To thine own self be true!" (Hamlet) But is true being true to yourself or following someone else's claims as truth... the Cause! "Fight for the Cause!" is the decree, "and defy yourself for the Cause! It will reward in the end!" So...who...what is right? How you do be a true person when you are unsure what is true? Oh God! Must I even experience the fear of extricating my true thoughts on paper because of the voices! The voices that say "Well, the Devil does not know your thoughts, but he hears you and sees you and wants to set the trap!" Well, what if I were to reply that *this* puts me in a trap! These voices that come from every side and every perspective always saying "Beware!" and "What if?!"...Such things just make me long to throw caution to the wind... recklessly!

01.28.2006

Lost the big V (12pm)

02.16.2006

So I lost it... it was inevitable. It had to happen; there was no way around it. Why? Was it because I couldn't wait? It was because I had to defy... shock them. It's pointless because they don't even know they are being shocked...How pathetic... I am pathetic and no one can tell the change... the difference.

Maybe he's right... Fuck the world.

02.26.2006

So many interruptions and crazy strange ones, too! First the church lady and her garbage cans. She even had the nerve to wave at me. Then the white van and a dude on a cell phone who Ricky didn't know. They weren't the brothers and then they drove away.

Later the cat in the window… talk about scaring the shit out of me! Like a creepy face in the darkness.

First I rated him (Ricky) and his finger talents an 8 or 9. But that changed to a 10! Wow! Oh yeah… and the muffins and how I had to bring them all the way back. They are the whole reason I am writing anything here anyway… or at least everything past the church lady part.

03.27.2006

Two days ago I was relieved to break up with him (Ricky). Now I am crying. Not necessarily because I want him back but because I am sure he believes I never loved him. I really did… in my heart I really do! I wasn't just fucking him, dammit! I was loving him! I was kissing his heart and the beautiful things about him that I believed in. Why does he have to be such a contradiction? I love him and I hate him!

09.11.2006

Where is my life in steps away from four years ago? Much more knowledge, for sure. Questions answered and wonderings affirmed. Questions I was unaware I even had.

I miss Dad, definitely, but I don't know what to think about him now. He is the past. He is almost a different world – a world that I have left behind. Slammed the door, but have been unable to throw the key away. I guess there is a small quiet yearning to return to that world. There was comfort and security there… as is afforded in any cage (smirk). I suppose I just want to step into the back doors to linger about… attempts to catch a glimpse or a scent of the person I used to be. A lost part of myself? Maybe to find out where I have hidden that spiritual, hungry, guided and guarded, vulnerable part of myself – past self. I don't even know what to call this person or personality I once was. However, I want to dig up this old me, I am afraid I have suppressed and buried it deep under anger and frustrated confusion. There is so much that I think I need to bring to the surface and face it, but I don't even know where to start or how – so I just step over it and ignore it. Momentarily at least.

I intended to make Rolando the topic of this entry. I intended to say he is amazing... and he is. He is too good to me and I don't understand why. I didn't want to admit this, but I am subconsciously expecting him to get bored or tired of me. Or I'm afraid I need him too much. The fact that he is there, offering to take care of me, to be a pillar I can lean on and an escape – it scares me. It is something I long for, I yearn for the stability but I fear it because what if it just falls out from under my feet?

On one hand I want to go to him, take up his offer and stay until I feel the urge to return. On the other hand... where did I find him? The kindness, sincerity, generosity, attention... it's all too good to be true. Aimee thinks I'm cold-hearted, I'm not. I'm hurt from Ricky and Brian, I just bury it inside. I step over that, too. But, oh God... I do not want it to happen again! This time I want to fall in love. I want to trust with all my heart and feel a dedication as strong as iron chains. I want to melt and die in him, give and take with him, walk together without the need of words. I want laughter and tears, anger and fears, beauty and bitterness, spilt all over and about us until we have stepped in and tasted of the vulnerability and strength of each other. I want him to fill me up 'til every other man shrinks to no comparison with him. I want to work beside him, to share his exhaustion until we have built something strong that rewards us each morning.

I am glad I have cried about this and truly felt the words that I write down here. I need to know that my heart is in this.

02.08.2007

Vegas. A faraway, fairytale sort of place that I never even had a slight desire to visit. Yet, now I live here? Well, officially for a week I have lived in this labyrinth of a city. Do I like it? Am I having fun? Am I scared? Hell, I don't know!

Rolando wants to buy me <<a shirt>>, probably custom made, that reads, "I don't know. I think so." Yeah, I guess that is me. Totally unsure. I don't feel at home here, and honestly, I didn't feel at home in Ontario, in Boise, or in the house on Amity.

I am wondering what happened to "home" in my life. I want to say it walked out the door... or was it stolen? When Dad died? But it bothers me to blame things on Dad's death, like it's feeling sorry for myself and I hate that.

02.19.2007

Not sure why the depression haunts me lately. Just seems to be there, stepping steadily behind me, reminding me of its presence whenever things grow silent and solemn. It's not debilitating at all and I don't feel sorry for myself. It's simply this nagging feeling that I have been trying to ignore because I am not sure I want to turn around and face it.

I wonder often if my problem is religious. I feel guilty and I want to talk to God, I think. I can't... honestly, I cannot! How do you communicate, even if it's one way, with something you are not sure you believe in? I think I believe in God in some sense, but the problem is I'm not sure on what grounds... not sure what I believe about Him and what he consists of. So, then I feel wrong to talk to Him until I have figured out what I believe. But how can I do that without talking to Him and discovering Him by His own way and not my own desires? I'm torn because there is so much pain, anger and confusion down the road of... well, what do I call it? Religion? Christianity?... maybe just Faith works?

If I diligently begin searching for God, I must dig, cut and pummel my way through that mess of my past mental manipulation. I must wisely sort through it, face the pain and face myself. I must seek to discover the right and retain it, and seek the wrong and discard it.

I have an honest fear, a huge fear, that I may discover something I don't like. I might discover a "truth" that I am not quite willing to embrace. It's this choking fear that I may find they are right and I am wrong and going back is my true salvation. But that just can't be. That would be death; heart rending, life-sucking death! No!

I have another problem. I'm not in love and I live with this man in a town far from home… or at least all that I have known. And I am only 20 years old. I believe I love him. I truly care for him but there is something missing. Maybe it's the wholeness of myself that is missing.

I haven't cried in awhile and it makes me feel inhuman. I'm just too empty, too tired to cry. I guess I'll try to figure it out later.

07.29.2007

It's been a long, crazy day. Started with church in long black slacks – feeling fresh and good. Music kinda sucked, but "covetousness does you no good" ☺ (Luke 14:12?) I can't quite remember.

Then there was Moxie Java with my good friend Izzy. Perfect. Even if he has old, dry food on his shirt… lol! Gotta love him ☺ Next, the discovery that my pictures have been deleted by some obvious ghost. Talk about pissed off! Mad, yes, very mad. "to have the audacity," I thought. As my MySpace bulletin said, "God couldn't have screwed their head on backwards during manufacturing, so it must have happened somewhere in shipping and handling." Then came the hot tub/movie invite. Here, things happened that weren't meant to happen, yet were inevitable and a little interesting. Made my stomach all queasy again and my hands a bit shaky. So, that all occurred crazy fast.

Then, I drive to the house to deliver invitations for my sister and the lady looks at me like she's never seen me before, but she was at my house like… last night? ☺ Whatever. Meanwhile, Rolando has been texting and begging but I just need some time to breathe. Finally, I make the call and once he has apologized about the pictures, explaining himself, and wearing me out, I just want to run, run and run or curl up and sleep…?

So, I get the pastels out – red, blue (that's the color I was feeling) black and yellow. I started with black, big curves connecting and then added straight, slashing yellow lines near sharp rising blue waves, with a touch of red dots and shading. Mom asked what it was "'cause Mom can't tell these things," she said. She is sweet. I let the tears fall and looked into her eyes and said, "I love you, Mama." Then I hung the picture up on the fridge with a magnet. The background is gray.

I suggest we eat out for a light dinner. Once there, I am informed by my old manager that Rolando had emailed a guest concern, reminiscing about August 14, 2006 – booth 53. How am I supposed to take this??? My mind says, "Leave me alone! Please stop!"

My mind is busy with that and I want to go for a walk with Mom and the dog… in the dusk, through empty parking lots. That was good. Mom is silly ☺ On the computer at home again; I see that people are stupid assholes again! My response and bulletin tell them like it is. I'm so sick of insecure, immature, ridiculous, drama-loving, shallow and dumbass mother fuckers! Fuck them! X 22!

I think I am chillin' out about that now, too. Wow. Haven't been this pissed in awhile – a long while. I got the phone call that I needed and now all I care about is my pillow, my black and white sheets and this amazing down comforter.

Author's Note:

I had met a second boyfriend, Rolando, while serving him at a local restaurant I was working at one Wednesday night, being single only a few months since dumping Ricky. I moved in with Rolando in Vegas after dating him for about four months long distance. I was there with him for about 7 months and then left him and went back home to live with my mother again. In this last entry, I had just returned home from leaving Rolando, and was fighting with him through cyberspace and telephone. A week or so later, I agreed to go on an already planned vacation with him for a week, and then I tried to cut him off from my life multiple times thereafter, for about a year. It was two months after writing this last entry that I met my current partner, Tomas, and began dating him. During those two months before meeting Tomas, I slept with multiple guys-friends and partied often. Upon meeting Tomas, we intended to just be like "friends with benefits," but we soon became jealous and it turned into... love?

I had first smoked weed with Ricky and did so a few times a week for the couple of months after I left church until I broke up with Ricky. About two or three times I smoked while dating Rolando because he knew I liked it, and he liked how sensual I became from it, so he found some from a friend. However, when I met Tomas, I soon found out he was very fond of weed and I basically became a pothead from that time on, trying a few other drugs in moderation with Tomas.

It's apparent that at this time I was struggling a lot with my Dad's death and therefore looking for men to replace him in my life. I was also struggling with a change in my world paradigm and trying to grow up without my family around. My mother was

*still in the church and I never felt I could confide in her. She
wouldn't understand from her perspective of the world.*

Excerpt Nine

06.01.1999

I give myself two thumbs up for today. Two big, fat thumbs up. Wow, I feel like I'm grown up...Sigh...

So here's what happened today. After finishing my English final for Mr. Thrash's class, I walked out to my car flooded with relief that I'd managed to make it through four years of high school, when Keisha walked up behind me, ranting about who knows what.

"Girl, someone is talking mad trash about you," she said snapping her neck from side to side, puckering out her lips at me.

I couldn't help but smile, I loved Keisha. She was so animated. She spoke her mind and didn't give two shits if you liked it or not, but if she liked you, and for some strange reason she happened to like me, she had your back.

"What do you mean? Who's talking shit?" I asked, trying to act like I cared. It was the last day of school and in the grand scheme of things it really didn't matter what anyone was saying. I would never see a fraction of the people in my senior class ever again...YAY...For four years I'd watched the pathetic comings and goings of the unrealistic kids in my school and that was way too long if you ask me.

"I don't know who it is, but they know a whole lot about you." Keisha said, snapped her fingers in a Z shape in front of my face. I laughed. She was really worked up.

"It's okay, school is over." I told her, continuing to walk toward my car. She walked with me. "What did you hear, that made you think I needed to know about it. People talk all the time. And I could care less."

"Girl, I wouldn't be saying that if I were you," she stopped walking and grabbed my arm. When I looked at Keisha's honey color eye's I could see she was worried. So it got me to thinking. She never gets worried about anything. In that way we were the same. So it hit me if Keisha was worried maybe I should be worried too...Great, just great!

I stopped next to my car and sat on the hood. "So tell me, what did you hear?"

"Well, my friend came up to me the other day, and I know she don't know you like me, and she started telling me how you lost your virginity on your back porch, and that when you and that guy you were dating all the way through school broke up, that you had break-up sex in the back yard on the grass."

That was all it took, I placed a hand on her arm and stopped her. She didn't have to say one more word. There was only one person who knew those things about me and she was headed my way. What were the odds? I squeezed Keisha's arm and nodded toward Rachel Pads. Nice last name right.

"What?" Keisha asked.

I pointed at the small black haired girl who looked all sweet and innocent. Yeah, right.

"It's her. Right there, walking toward us." I told Keisha loud enough for Rachel to hear me. To make sure she knew I was talking to her.

Keisha gasped, "No fucking way. What are you going to do?" she said perking up. I could tell she thought she had a front row seat to a fight.

Rachel Pads was what you called a chronic liar or sociopath.

I waited for her to come closer. I wanted to see if she had the balls to talk to me. She thought she was tough. Truth was everyone was fooled, but me.

I could feel hate boiling inside me. I should've listened to Leda. When Rachel and I started to become friends, Leda pulled me aside and said to watch my back around Rachel because she was a black widow spinning her web around everyone. At the time I didn't understand. I should've known better. It's never good when someone tells you something like that.

I watched Rachel move closer. My adrenaline was pumping. For a fraction of a second the image of me pounding her face in consumed me. I fisted my hands. I was going to do it. I was going to beat the shit out of her. What made her think she had the right to share my business with the whole school? She was the school slut, the one who lied and told people she had a brother that killed himself to make them feel sorry for her. When the truth was, she was an only child. She was the one who turned everything you said around to hurt people. I'd been through hell and back with my high school sweetheart. I mean damn, the wounds were still gaping holes and here she was driving another knife into my chest. I dragged in a deep breath and pushed it out slowly.

Keisha crossed her arms over her chest as Rachel came to a stop in front of me. "You a stupid little girl aren't you." she said, giving Rachel the stink eye.

"What?" Rachel replied, looking at me all surprised. Like how on earth could this girl be mean to her? It was easy to hate someone who didn't give a shit about you or your feelings as long as it amused her. Rachel was very manipulative and cold as ice.

"Don't, what me, little girl, I'll slap you four shades of blue." Keisha was face to face with her now. I slid off the hood and pulled Keisha out of the way. This wasn't her fight.

"I don't remember starting a conversation with you." I said to Rachel.

Her eyes went wide.

"You were talking about me," she said, "I heard you."

"That's right. I was. I was just telling my friend Keisha here that you're the stupid bitch that has been spreading my personal business to the entire school."

"I don't know what you're talking about," Rachel said, the corners of her mouth pulled tight.

It was a hidden smile, that wasn't so hidden. Oh, that was it. I was going to sock her in the nose.

I got a bad feeling in my gut. What was she trying to do? I mean really. Why start trash talking two days before we graduated?

I stepped up and hovered over Rachel, my fists clenched tight. I glared at her. But there was something in her eyes that made me crank my brain into high gear. Rachel didn't do anything without a motive. What could she gain if I beat the shit out of her? Then it came to me like a low creeping fog. If I was mad enough to fight her, which I was, she would go to the principal and stop me from getting to walk tomorrow at graduation.

DING, DING, DING, we have a winner!

I pulled a fist back ready to launch it at Rachel's face. She slammed her eyes shut. Smiling, I stepped back, taking her in. She was seriously pathetic. Keisha just stared at me. I crossed my arms over my chest, and said, "I'm so glad you think my business is worthy of school gossip. Wow, I have hit the big time now. Thanks you're the best."

Rachel's eyes popped open, face going slack. Keisha burst out laughing, doing a crazy dance beside me. I really didn't know what was better. The look of sheer disappointment on Rachel's face, knowing I beat her at her own game or Keisha's crazy dance.

Rachel turned and climbed into her car and drove off.

Keisha was still laughing.

"Girl, that was some funny shit. Did you see her face? It was like you just stole her favorite dance move." She gave me a hug, looked me in the eyes and said, "See you tomorrow."

I watched Keisha rush off toward the bus stop and I thought to myself...yes, yes you will.

Authors Note:

This was the first time in my life I actually wanted to inflict bodily harm. To this day, I'm happy I don't sink that low. This girl Rachel had some serious issues and I'm sad to say they never improved.

http://www.thesecretlivesofpeople.com

Excerpt Ten

12.11.2011

It was so weird. I don't know what happened. I hated you. Couldn't stand you. Asked everyone in our community to keep you away from me. The sight of you repulsed me. And then....today. Today at dance. I don't know what happened. All of a sudden I felt it. Felt this rush of sexual energy pouring off you but not really off of you… it was more like it was generating back and forth between the two of us. I remember after dance I was sitting there talking to Ana and you came up to me and playfully wrestled me to the ground. You laid on top of me and it turned me on so much. Chris was there and he was like, "I never want to hear you bitch about him again" because he saw how turned on I was by you because my nipples got hard (I guess) when you laid on me.

I guess it started awhile ago at the firewalk. Well, it started way before that but at the firewalk you thought I was pretty bad-ass because I walked on the broken glass. Now…looking back, I am not so sure if you really thought I was bad ass or if it was more like you didn't want to look like a pussy for not walking the glass so you walked it just to prove how fucking manly you are…..anyway, I digress, diary. The point is that, oh, I don't know, at the firewalk in November, when I was still with Jonathan, you claimed to be impressed by the fact that I had the balls to walk on the glass AND the hot coals. Yeah. So? You also know that I am a fighter and a warrior. I think this turned you on more than anything. It turned you on, probably still does, that I am the only person in this community who has had the balls to stand up to you. Everyone else is too afraid to because they can't see through you like I can. You are really just a big fucking coward, aren't you? A coward who hides behind your shield of strength but I know that shield is only a shield; it's a façade. I see who you really are, Kataro. Fucking coward. Again….I digress.

So….back to the events at hand: When breakfast was ready I went downstairs. You were sitting there. I went up to you and said, "I think we should just do it and get it over with". You said, when, I said, today. Later today. And we did. I went over and we fucked and it was by far the best sex I have ever had. It was raw sex. Animalistic sex. Primal. I was shocked, really. The man I hated. The man whose very presence repulsed me was now pleasuring me far more than any other man I have ever known. How could this be possible? I am totally blown away.

It was incredible. He was so gentle, so romantic, so passionate and so primal all at the same time. I can't wait to do it again. And, oh my god, does he know a woman's body. I am really not a multiple orgasm type of woman but this man, this man, can make me cum over and over again. How utterly fantastic. And what a pleasant surprise. I thought he was such a dick, but he is actually really incredible. I am so happy that I don't hate him anymore.

03.2.2012

Fucking prick. I can't fucking stand you. Everything about you disgusts me. The thought of you repulses me and makes me sick to my stomach. What the hell was I thinking? How could I have allowed you to touch me for two months? OH MY GOD…..I think I am going to be sick.

You disgust me. There is nothing redeemable about you. You are fat, stupid, and a raging alcoholic who has no clear perception of himself or of reality. I cannot believe I tolerated your bullshit as long as I did.

Are you kidding me? I am so angry at myself. I cannot believe I fucked an overweight Mexican who professes to be Native American, dude. Gross. I am so grossed out now. I am plotting ways to take revenge on you. I can't believe I allowed you to speak so horribly to me and to demean me. You? Demean me? Please. Look at you mother fucker and then look at me. You talk about young college girls well, the difference is this: hear it and weep. The difference is this: young college girls would laugh or throw up at the thought of having sex with you. Young college boys? Young college boys, however, would line up to fuck me. That is the difference. I am hot. I am desirable. You are not. That is why you had to ask me every mother fucking day if I was seeing anyone else. Every day, Kataro. Sometimes more than once. Hell, sometimes more than twice. Every day we had to go through this and do you know why? Because you know I am hot and I could have those young college boys if I wanted to.

You are a loser. I hate you. What? Did you put a spell on me or something? How on earth did I go from being repulsed by you, to wanting you, back to complete repulsion?

Oh and then you deleting my number and then texting and calling my best friend to get it back? Hahahahahahahahahaha hahahahahahahahahaha......the joke's on you, isn't it? Big fucking baby throwing a tantrum and deleting my number only to regret it the next day. You will never have it now. And I am so, so glad.

03.14.2012

It has been two weeks. The anger is consuming me. I find myself laying awake at night plotting your demise. I want to say something really mean to you. Want to send you a really nasty message on Facebook. You know, one of those hit-below-the-belt messages. But I won't. I keep telling myself to take the high road and not sink to your level.

It has been two weeks and I have not heard from you nor seen you around in the community. Thank god. I fear I may throw up if I run into you.

Yet….that was really, really good sex. I will write about the sex another time. Hard to describe it other than it was like opening a portal to another world. It was like dying and being 100% completely alive all at the same time. Yet, it was killing me. Sucking me. Draining me of my life energy while at the same time feeding me. I remember going into the gym at the Y one night after we had sex. Every man, Kataro. Every fucking man, young, old, white, black, brown, handicapped, disabled, looked at me. Every single one of them. Talk about feeling powerful.

I miss that. I miss what you unleashed in me.

Author's Note:

This is about a man who was my lover for two months. Our sexual relationship was, and still is, I suppose, volatile, unhealthy, dysfunctional, electric, exciting, stimulating, refreshing and dangerous all at the same time. He was a man that I was interested in over a year before we actually got together. I knew the sex with him would be phenomenal, and it was. I have a sense for things like that. After we got together, it quickly turned into a nightmare. The man is an alcoholic and he lured me into his alcoholic nightmare. He became verbally and physically abusive.

Excerpt Eleven

02.27.2007

Today has to have been one of the worst decisions I've ever made. Not that any of the ones I've made have been any good either. Least of all the one I've been continuing to make in attempting to date Corbett. He's married for gawd's sake! For everything in me that's broken, I truly believed that he loved me. Now, after I've found out that I'm pregnant with his child, he's nowhere near. No, wait! I know where he is. He's home, with his WIFE!!!

I've had to take $500 out of my tax return and spend it on a chemical abortion to remove the fetus before it develops any further. Corbett told me that he would pay for half of it. I believe him, but I'm not sure if I'll ever see the money. He's not exactly rolling in dough. Maybe someday, I'll get half of it back. The bottom line is that I was able to afford this right now.

I had to go in and get an exam, then afterwards, I got escorted into the doctor's office and he gave me the rundown on what was going to happen. It didn't seem that there was going to be anything really out of the ordinary to worry about. After the lecture and info drop, he gave me this little cup with a pill in it. I was to consume the pill and then head home. I asked Brian to come with me because I wasn't sure how it was going to affect me.

Such a simple act to obliterate such a seemingly unoffensive being. However, this life would absolutely ruin many others. This child cannot be brought into this world. I can't afford to support another baby. Corbett sure as hell wouldn't be around to help me out at all and if his wife ever found out that he'd had a baby with another woman, I'm fairly certain my life would be in jeopardy.

Now, down to the experience. I was told that once I got home, I was to lay in bed and allow the chemicals to kick in. Well, I did that and I felt the most horrible cramps I've ever felt. They seemed a lot like the labor pains when I was having Aunyah. After all, I would imagine that's exactly what's happening. My body is expelling the fetus just as it would be laboring a full-term infant.

Laying in bed, I stood up and had to run to my bathroom. Once I got there, I couldn't get my clothing off fast enough and ended up getting blood all over the toilet, the bathtub, the rug, my towels, up my arms, and all over my hands. I had to stay on the toilet and in the bathroom for almost an hour. The whole time, I'm crying uncontrollably because of the pain and shock of seeing all the blood everywhere and knowing it's all mine. Brian kept coming to the door to check on me. I wouldn't open the door for him, so I'm sure he was worried about me. I think I probably should have left the door unlocked and allowed him to help me, but I also think that I deserve to go through this alone.

Here's the clincher. It would be somewhat bearable had I not spent all that time bawling, only to decide it might be better to bawl in bed, under the covers. So I stood up and began to clean myself. The doctor told me that I would experience large amounts of blood clots. So, when I was cleaning up, I saw many of them. One of which I was entirely unprepared to deal with. This clot was larger and more solid than any of the others so I opted to investigate.

That was a huge mistake. The mass I had mistakenly thought was another blood clot was actually the expelled fetus that had come from my uterus. Right there in my hand was the baby I'd created. Now, that child was incontrovertibly deceased. There wasn't any way for me to go back and change my mind, not that I would have, given the circumstances.

This realization and seeing the baby in my hand gave way to a whole new wave of hysterical tears which also brought Brian to the door to inquire as to my condition. It surprises me that, considering what I was doing to myself and another human, someone still cared enough for me to be concerned for my welfare.

I stared at the dead baby on the toilet paper in my hand for quite some time. Curiosity and grief prevented me from immediate discard. I examined it like a doctor with both medical interest and shame in my mind. Finally, I came to the point mentally where it was time to let go. It was time to face the stark reality of what I had done and I needed to allow myself to move forward. I folded the toilet paper gingerly over the dead fetus as though my gentle touch with the paper would give the child any type of comfort in the afterlife. I lowered the bundle to the toilet and allowed it to drop from my fingers into the water.

For quite a long time I pondered whether or not to take the baby out and bury it in the ground. Alas, I decided that the best way to deal with this situation was to remove all physical memory of the occurrence. So I reached for the handle and flushed the toilet. Flushed all of the blood and tears I'd shed. Flushed a great deal of my pride and self-respect down the drain. Broken, torn, and traumatized I picked up what mess I could manage through the cascade of tears that had burst anew.

Slowly I made my way out of the bathroom and onto my bed. Under my blanket, I broke down again. Crying uncontrollably, unable to recognize that there was someone else in the room, I allowed myself to grieve. Here I am now. Opting to relive the oh-so-new emotions and trauma through text. The only way I know to express myself fully, through words on paper.

Brian is sitting on the end of my bed, quietly and patiently. He's waiting for me to come out of my stupor and tell him I'm ok. The thing is, I'm not ok. I'm not going to be ok. This is something that will be with me and haunt me for the rest of my life. I cannot undo it and I can't make it right.

The most difficult part about this whole process is not the pain. It's not the copious amounts of blood everywhere. It's the mental anguish of essentially deleting a child I never get to meet. Regardless of the circumstances, it is still a child that was created by two people. One of which, the carrier, is me.

I am certainly pro-choice, but that does not make this choice any easier for myself. It is such a simple act to just decide that a baby would cause my world, which is already precariously perched on the precipice of an abyss, to completely collapse. I'm trying to figure out whether I'm more concerned about the possible repercussions on my life, or on Corbett's. You'd think that with the situation and his behavior, that I wouldn't care about how it might affect him. The bottom line is, I love that man. I hate him sometimes because of the situation and circumstances both he and myself have gotten into.

I despise the fact that it's Brian sitting here hoping to hear from me, instead of the man that helped me create this mess. Not two months ago, he told me he was done with his marriage and that we were together. I knew better, but I just couldn't stop myself from allowing the fall. Less than 2 days later, his wife called him and he went running back to her. I was and still am crushed. He showed me with so few actions that I meant so very little to him and yet, when I am most vulnerable, I want his company. I have this friend here, who's seen me through many of that man's excruciating emotional blows, and yet, I want not his company.

As much as I need to write this out, I need desperately to allow myself to rest and attempt to recover physically from this endeavor. If I've got the energy and thought to write, I will continue this tomorrow.

03.13.2007

I've noticed that I've been experiencing some rather disturbing new outbursts lately. These aren't outbursts of temper. In fact, I'm not sure what these are at all.

When I was on Deborah's team, I started noticing that I wasn't able to see the stats screen. And then, shortly thereafter I started having these spells where I couldn't focus on anything, I would get supremely dizzy, and my arm would start jerking uncontrollably.

Well, now I've been hauled to the ER more times than I can count because the arm jerking became whole-body. I changed teams in February and go figure, my first couple of weeks there were coupled with morning sickness. Now, I'm having concerns that I'm going to lose my job because I can barely sit at my desk without getting so frustrated with myself that I reel into another of what I've come to call seizures.

This last time I was sent to the ER, the doctor who came to attend told me that I needed to stop what I was doing. He said that I was doing this to myself and that it was my fault. I was thinking, "Really?! You think I'd want to be going through all of this? You think I enjoy racking up all of these bills that there's no freaking way I'll be able to pay? You think I want my daughter to see me flopping like a fish daily?"

Aunyah has walked in on me a number of times and I've had to have her go get me help. Really? Having an 18 month-old go get help for her mother? This is getting absolutely unbearable. First the crap with Corbett, then the procedure, and now this? I don't know how much more of this I can take. I've been regularly considering how much easier it would be if I didn't have to deal with any of this. It would be much easier on all of my friends and my daughter if I just weren't here.

http://www.thesecretlivesofpeople.com

A light in the dark here would be the fact that I've had some attention from a gentleman I never thought would even look at me a second time. His name is Chris and he works at DirecTV with me. He's not on my team but he comes in an hour after my team and leaves a little bit later.

I spent a great deal of time staring at him whenever I could and caught him looking back at me a few times as well. Then, I wanted to find out what his name was so I started asking around to see if anyone on my team knew him. One of the chicks did and then word got over to him that I wanted to know who he was. So, he walked over to me on his break and dropped me a note saying that his name was Chris. He told the dude next to me that when a beautiful woman wants to know your name, you take the time to introduce yourself.

I have been quite giddy ever since, but the problems with my health are really weighing on my mind right now. We'll see where things go from here. Hopefully up.

Author's Note:

Today, I'm much further in life than I ever thought possible. Brian was my best friend's boyfriend and also a roommate in the apartment we were renting. He was a very close friend of mine until we all moved out and went our separate ways. I am no longer in touch with him, though I greatly miss his friendship.

Corbett remained with his wife and is still with her to this day. He did eventually reimburse me for half of the cost of the abortion. We have completely lost touch and I am happy for that because I am quite ashamed to say that I have been someone's mistress.

With regard to Chris, he and I dated for several years thereafter and had a little boy together in 2009, although we are not together anymore. He has left the state and refuses to pay child support.

As for the seizures, after blood analysis, EKGs, an EEG, x-rays, sleep analysis, an MRI, a psychological evaluation and numerous trips to the Emergency room, I remain without answers. On one occasion within the ER, I was told that I was putting myself through these seizures and that I needed to cease the behavior. To this day, I still experience this severe response to over-powering stress. The only conclusion any medical professional has made is that these may be a form of panic/anxiety attack. Nonetheless, I am not in control of it and I wish I was.

I have been through many traumatic events, but they all have created the person I am now. I am an excellent mother and a compassionate friend! I have a great family that has been very supportive of me no matter how many mistakes I've made.

Please note that if you are pro-choice, pro-life, or on the fence, it would do you a great justice to take into consideration what one woman has been through in the face of such a morally-defunct decision. Many question the reasons behind women choosing to eliminate a life. The choice is not easy and the repercussions are many! What I have gone through has stuck with me even after all this time. Re-living the experience is something that breaks my heart over and over again. I weep when I consider what I've done, and yet I cannot change anything about what has already happened. So I have to keep on living and come someday, I need to allow myself forgiveness for such a decision.

Excerpt Twelve

07.28.2011

Oh my god, so I was like checking my email and talking to this guy Scott that I know and we were kind of flirting and what not and then all of a sudden, out of the blue, a chat message pops up from you. From you, Alex. It was cute. You said, "Hi!" I said, "Hi, stranger," at which point you apologized for being such a stranger and for not being able to make our last coffee date due to your work schedule. You asked me what I was doing tonight. It was a Saturday night. I didn't have any plans. I said, "I don't know. What are you doing?" You said, or wrote, really, since it was on the email Google chat, that you were rehearsing but should be done soon. You asked if I had time to get together. Ba-bum. That was the sound of my heart beating out of my chest. I am so crazy about you, what do you mean do I have time to get together? Of course I do, but, wait….I gotta act cool. Act casual. So that is what I did. Cool. Casual. I nonchalantly replied, if nonchalant can be picked up in an email I am not sure, that I thought I was free but would have to double check. You said ok and to call you in about an hour. I waited 'til like an hour and ten. I called. You picked up right away. I could hear the anticipation in your voice. I was super excited and nervous. I talk a lot when I get excited and nervous so, I was talking a lot. We agreed to meet at a local tea house. You wanted to meet soon. I said I was sweaty from being out in the sun all day and wanted to take a quick shower. You said not to worry about it. You had been working all day.

So…we met at Shangri La tea house. It went well. I love talking to you. You are smart and we have a lot in common. Most men bore me. You are not boring. Not only do you know a lot about theater but about philosophy and life in general. You started talking about how you were looking up at the stars one day and how you felt so small....and, well, I can't remember the rest but I remember how I felt when you were talking about it. It was like how I felt that day in viewpoints when you read the poem about the squirrel. It was at that moment....at that precise moment, when you read that poem, that my entire world stood still and everything around me just slowed down. All I could see was your lips moving and I could feel you. Feel your passion, feel your pain, feel your joy. It was at that moment, when you read the squirrel poem, that I knew I was falling in love with you.

It was like that at Shangri La when you were talking about the stars. Something about the way your eyes look when you look at me. The way you look into me. The way your eyes, you search me out.

At tea, you insinuated that you wanted to have sex with me. You said something to the effect of: I wonder what it would be like to be attracted to someone and want to have sex with her yet not be able to. Tonight is the night that I found out you are married. I did not know that before. You're married. Wow. Imagine that. Sigh. Mirrors crashing, world shattering, violins playing a tragic tune in A minor.

After our tea and appetizer we walked outside and continued talking. My daughter was having a tragic moment with her boyfriend so I had to leave quickly. You held my gaze. You kept engaging me in conversation. Not being rude or anything cuz you knew I had to leave....relating to the tragedy my daughter was experiencing. God Alex, I just fall for you more and more. The more I get to know you the more I adore you. I started to walk away and said, "I have to get home to my child." You said, "I often wonder what it would be like to have sex with you." I said, "And I want to have sex with you, too, Alex." Then I mentioned something about being disappointed that you are married. Awkward silence. Then you said, "Well, now that it is out, it is awkward now." I said that it didn't have to be and that when you were ready I would be there. In fact, I called you on the way home and reiterated that and told you that I had wanted you for a long time and that I would be here when you are ready.

You didn't call me back.

10.02.2011

So there is this song. It says, "I waited for you.....today." I was going to start this piece like that but didn't want to sound like some cheesy top-40 song. But it's true. I waited for you. Well maybe not entirely true. I didn't actually wait for you, but I did, in a sense. Wait, I mean. I waited for you to call me back.

On Tuesday you called me. That is right. You called me motherfucker. I didn't call you. You called me to say thank you for coming to your play. You called me to ask if I had any free time this week. I said I had Friday available. You said that Friday was fine. I told you that I did African dance and yoga in the morning. You said to call you when I was free. I called you when I was free. Got your voicemail. I left a message telling you that I was free and would be all day until about 3:00 p.m. I knew you would not return my call. I could feel it.

I was really excited. I even went to Plato's Closet and went dress shopping. I wanted to look nice for you. Didn't really find anything there but. . . I went dress shopping. For you. To look nice. For you.

My daughter has this really sexy dress that I bought for her on one of my trips to San Francisco. I called my daughter and asked her if I could borrow her dress from San Francisco for my date on Friday. I was so excited. I got my hair done. I wanted to look pretty. For you. It went right to voicemail.

I even planned how it would go. I planned what we would talk about. I thought about how awesome our conversation would be. I thought about how we would talk about your wife and son and how any kind of "us" could ever be possible. I thought about how much I wanted to touch you and kiss you but mostly how much I wanted to talk and share ideas and thoughts with you. I was so excited. It went right to voicemail.

10.25.2011

I saw you today. It has been over a month. I saw you quite by accident, really. My daughter. She was late coming out of the theater class that you teach her. I text her asking her where she was. She didn't answer. I called her. She didn't answer. I did not want to go in. I knew that I would see you. Face to face. With you. It went right to voicemail.

My body was shaking. For several reasons, really. I did not know where my daughter was so I was shaking because I was fearful for her safety. That was one reason. The second: I knew the minute I got out of my car and walked up the stairs to the building that I would be there face to face with you. Shaking for two specific yet distinct reasons. It was an interesting kind of tremor, really. A shake not quite like any other I had experienced. Fear, nervous for my child's well-being wondering if she was still in there because I saw all of the other kids leaving, then thoughts of well, what if she is not in there and she has left, and then I come face to face with you and I don't know where my child has gone, combined with oh shit what if she is in there talking with you and I walk in and am face to face with you. A no win situation for me either way. Either way I would be face to face with you. With you and your masks. With you and your bullshit. With you and your pathetic excuses. With you and your sorrow. With you and your trapped soul.

I forced my body to move through the tremors and go to find my girl.

The building was quiet on the first floor. Ghostly. Empty. Vacant. Beautiful and decorated but empty. Like you. Like your trapped soul. Like the mask of sanity and well-being that you wear. I know what is under that mask, Alex. I see you. I see into the real you. That is why you fear me.

No one around. I walked down the stairs. Nothing. Just like you. Just like what you did for me. Nothing. It went right to voicemail. I dressed up. For you. Heart pounding now really worried about my girl. I walked to the rehearsal room. I saw you first. No, actually I heard you first. I continued walking toward the sound of your voice. I stopped at the entrance of the doorway. Your back was turned to me. I saw my beautiful angel behind you. I could tell by what was being said, what you were saying, that she had confided in you. You were advising her. She needed you to advise her. I needed you to answer the phone.

I stood there for a moment to listen. Your back was turned to me. You felt me there. You stopped talking. I stood silently still. Everything became very still. Time stopped. That is how I knew that you knew that I was standing there. Behind you. In the stillness. You felt me. We felt each other. Nothing moved. No breath was released. I sensed your awareness of me. Like an animal you sensed my invisible presence. Felt me. Smelled me.

My child did not see me. I turned and walked away. I wanted to give her the chance to talk with you. It is what she needed. Male advice. Male influence. She adores you.

I sat down on the couch in the other room. The air conditioner was blowing so all I could here were muffled voices. The air conditioner stopped. You were talking to my child about love. I heard you say that it was the most powerful thing in the universe. I heard you say, to my child, how you longed for love more than anything. I heard you say it was the most important thing. I heard you say it is what we live for. I heard you talking to my daughter about your wife. It went right to voicemail.

I was sitting on the couch. You walked into the room. My daughter was behind you. You saw me. You did not look surprised that I was sitting there. Out there on the couch in the other room. You heard me before. You sensed my presence. You knew I was there. You came over to me immediately. You asked how I was doing and put your arm around me in an attempt to hug me. I stiffened up and let you half hug me. I turned my body into you slightly. Heart carefully guarded. You kept it to the one-armed lame hug. You pulled away and made a feeble attempt at small talk. I stood there. Face to face. With you. It was awkward as fuck. No one knew what to say. You asked me how I've been. I said I have been well. Then we just stood there facing each other with what seemed like an eternity. No one knew what to say. Finally I said, "I am working with Jack in debate" You said, "Oh, really?" and that was that. More ridiculous small talk walking up the stairs but not a lot. In your eyes....what? Vacancy. Nothing. Desire well hidden. Longing for love – forgotten.

You look like shit, Alex. So unhealthy. So thin. What happened? I did not see any light in your eyes. It went right to voicemail. I dressed up. For you. I wanted to share my love. With you. I only wanted to make you feel good. To elevate you to new forms of ecstasy that you have never experienced before.

It was awkward. You said, "I haven't seen you in ages." You could have seen me. You did not pick up the phone. You did not call me back. You did not respond to my multiple attempts to contact you. To talk. To talk through whatever. We could have been lovers. We could have shared our bodies. Our minds. Our souls. We could have merged energies. "I haven't seen you in ages" it is almost comical, ludicrous really. And then you act like you are so happy to see me yet all the while I see the pain in your face. I see how a loveless existence has deteriorated your body and soul while I listen to you stream all of that bullshit about love to my teenage daughter when you are such a hypocrite because you say love is all that you care about yet you turn away from it when it is right in front of you Alex Hayward. What the fuck happened to you? You look like hell. You speak the words but words are all you have. I could activate you. You feel that from me. You want that from me. You fear that from me. Don't pretend with me. It does not become you, but, oh, yeah, that's right....you are an actor. I forgot.

I dressed up. For you. It went right to voicemail. Face to face with you.

10.31.2011

– and now for something different.....

I dressed up for you.

It is Halloween night. I am home alone. My almost 20-year-old oldest child is hunting with her fiancée and his family in Idaho City. She sent me a text. It said, "Help me! Screaming kids and screeching Chihuahuas!" She is funny. I miss her. I went over to her house and we sat in her back yard yesterday and talked.

It is Halloween night.

I am home alone. I bet you, you, Alex, are trick-or-treating with your wife and son, aren't you? Maybe making caramel apples together or something oh so fucking sweet like that with your cozy fucking family, probably even sitting by a warm fire and drinking hot cocoa....oh now isn't that precious, but me? Me? No...I am here.....all alone. A fucking knock-out, beautiful, powerful, sexual woman with a body to die for home alone while you are with your frumpy fucking overweight wife I am HOME ALONE...DO YOU HEAR ME YOU MOTHER FUCKER???? DO YOU FUCKING

HEAR ME? You really shouldn't go around saying you want to have sex with someone and then never answer her calls or text messages and then pretend like nothing is going on. DON'T YOU KNOW HOW MUCH THAT HURT ME? Still hurts me?

My youngest child is 16. She is trick-or-treating or something like that with her boyfriend. They have been together for 8 months. I think it is serious. My baby is leaving me. She is separating. Cutting the umbilical cord, the spiritual, maternal, mother-daughter attachment to me more and more every day. It is normal. It is what she should do.

When I pulled into my driveway this evening memories flooded me – the hustle and bustle of Halloweens past and frantically rushing around getting kids into costumes, carving pumpkins at the last minute (hey mom weren't we supposed to do this BEFORE Halloween night?), the house was all lit up with our Halloween decorations. In fact the entire decorating process was a big deal, an all day ordeal, and we usually did it on October 1st. This year I decorated alone. And kids rushing, running through the neighborhood, our house an endless stream of neighborhood kids screaming trick or treat and mine, well, so excited...I remembered the year I was with Mike and we all got dressed up. Kevin & Luke were with us. Lucinda was a devil. That costume cost a fortune. Mike had just sold his house so we had a lot of money. We went to a party first then trick or treating and then memories of going to Haunted World, the corn maze, Linder Farms, the pumpkin patch and the excitement and frustration of getting everybody ready and then out the door and, oh, yeah, can't forget watching creepy movies and the X-Files every Halloween night. Tonight it is quiet. My porch light is burnt out. A knock on the door. One single trick or treater stands there. Alone. Trick or treat. I give him candy. Thank you. Have a great night. Etc, etc.

And then there was Harrison Blvd. That was last year. Last year on Harrison then to the Co-Op for ice cream. We sat in the parking lot and ate it. Lucinda, Brianna, Matt and me. Then I drove them to other neighborhoods. This year I am alone. She has a boyfriend now. I think it is serious. Oh and I remember how much of an ordeal the whole month of October used to be. The kids would tease me because it was the only time I would really get into baking and cooking. I would make Halloween treats of all kinds, cupcakes, chocolate pizzas, colored pudding and Jello treats, etc. And we would have parties....we did that last year too. And all the Halloween parades at the schools and parties and cupcakes and spooky fun. Remember the creepy masks that we got at Big Lots and they were all only like a dollar a piece and then we used them to make a haunted "shed" in the back yard and all the kids screamed and Hailey was crying and you got mad at me cuz I was trying to be scary but you said I was stupid? Probably cuz I am your mom. And then the bobbing for apples went bad because the water spilled all over the garage and then it smelled like cat piss, oh and last year taking pictures of you all in the grass and Kristina said it was a porno in progress and creepy Shane was here and nobody knew why, and he wanted to watch me swing on the pole and take pictures to send to his friend (yeah....creepy), and then Lowell showed up uninvited wearing some creepy mask. That was the night I broke my four month celibacy phase but maybe that is irrelevant here and now....now....this year....I feel nothing. Numb. It is like October came and went and omg it is Halloween already? What happened? I am apathetic. Enthusiasm seems like such an effort.

I dressed up for you. It went right to voicemail. You never called me back. You never came back. My father never came back. My husband never came back. You. You Alex. You never came back.

Entry who-cares....

I think I am okay. I think I am doing okay and then I see you. I see your fucking face and I realize that I am not okay - nothing is okay and I have just become hard and closed my heart again and didn't even realize it and the reason that it has closed down is because of men like you. Men who toy with it play with it toss it around like it is just a fucking ball of yarn that kittens play with. And then you have the audacity to look so fucking good and so healthy and so beautiful. It was easier for me to deal with not having you when you looked sick and then I see you and I realize that I envy you and what have I done with my life? Nothing. I am trapped. Trapped as a single mother. Trapped as a professor. Trapped making no money living in endless poverty having sex with men for money just so I can have money to take care of my child but it is not enough. It is never enough and I see you and I realize how pathetic my life is and how pathetic I have become and how I am doing nothing worthwhile. I hang with all the new age freaks that I don't even like, except Dosha, of course. I am crazy about him. I see you and my heart opens again whether I like it or not. I try to be rude to you. I am a little rude to you. I just think about you and your wife and son at home so loyal waiting for you and you doing your plays and directing and acting and living out your dream and being completely fulfilled by your career and I just want to sleep all day because I cannot face the dreariness of my life anymore. I was dating and fucking someone with Asperger's for god's sake and one of your actors texts me and is totally into me or so it seems and I am so very tired of being unfulfilled and searching for that man who is worthy of me and who will shower me with everything and then you have to say you owe me a text, several texts really, and then say you will take me out for a beer and I say I don't drink and you say okay, "coffee" then you remember I don't drink coffee either so you say "tea."

I'll buy you tea"…but I know you won't. I have heard that before Alex. I will not hold my breath…and why do you have to hug me and look at me?

I felt good about things until I saw you. I want to be a part of something bigger like a play as intense and brilliant as that was. I want to feel a sense of belonging in a community. I want to be surrounded by intellectual artistic people instead of the new age uneducated ones I surround myself with and I want my body to be adored by someone who is truly in love with me and sees me….not just my body.

Author's Note:

This series of journal entries is about a man that I thought I had very strong feelings for and thought I was in love with. He was my daughter's drama teacher and, at one point, my drama teacher. The "viewpoints" mentioned in the piece was the drama technique that he was teaching adults. I developed strong feelings for him over the course of two years. The entries only cover a portion of our relationship. I found out that he was married after about a year of knowing him. As of this date, March 11, 2012, I still have feelings for him. I haven't seen him in over three months. However, my daughter says that he still asks about me.

Excerpt Thirteen

May 1st

I woke up with my head splitting this morning and tried my damndest to figure out just what had happened last night. All I knew at first was that when I woke up there were clothes strung from hell to breakfast, and Robert was curled up next to me in the bed. When I went to the living room memories started to flood back of the night before. Troy was asleep on the couch and that's when it hit me. The dinner, too many shots of tequila. We wobbled our way back to the house and that's when it started. First it was only Robert touching me but then I remembered Troy and Robert both touching me and undressing me. Me undressing them. Oh hell what have I done! I can remember feeling both their hands on me and at one point I can remember feeling the pain and excitement as I rode on top of Robert with him in my pussy and then Troy entering my ass from behind. No wonder I woke up feeling like my ass was on fire. I do remember it was the most insane orgasm I have ever had. I need a fucking Alka Seltzer while I try to piece things back together.

Later that day

Well if I wasn't going to be able to remember Robert and Troy sure weren't going to let me forget. While I cooked them breakfast they went over the details from last night. They kept saying how hot it was and how much they wanted to do it again. They both talked about their favorite parts. For Robert it was when I was on my knees sucking his cock while troy fucked me from behind. For Troy it was when they both had me one in each hole and were riding me hard. As they were talking about it I was feeling shame, but at the same time I felt a funny twinge in my pussy. They want to do it again next Saturday. I told them I'd think about it. I just don't know because it feels so dirty and nasty but at the same time it's one of the most erotic things I have ever experienced.

May 4th

I just got home from work and am exhausted. I'm getting a little pissed at Robert because it seems like the only thing he can talk about is the ménage a trois. It's like he's obsessed by it. I get that it was out of this world but damn man, I can't believe on a certain level he could share me so easily with another man and not get the slightest bit concerned that I may jump ship and leave him for Troy. I don't understand men at all! I am having a lot of fucking trepidation about going through this again. The more he keeps talking about it the more I just want to tell him to stick it!

May 7th

Well I just finished getting dressed and am waiting for the boys to show. I decided to go through with it. Robert took me shopping for a set of thigh highs and a pair of unbelievable spike heels that I absolutely love. I'm having a glass of wine and trying to stop the butterflies from flitting around in my stomach. I hope I don't live to regret this!

May 8th

It was way more erotic this time because I managed to maintain some sobriety. I drank enough wine to help loosen me up but not enough to put me over the edge. We got to the club and picked a booth way at the back of the club. Thank goodness it was dark because if anyone could have seen what Troy and Robert were doing to me under the table we would have gotten thrown out. The club had a really nice blues band going but I can hardly remember any of the music for what they were doing to me. Robert and Troy were reaching under my dress and stroking me. Robert would be stroking my clit and Troy would be sticking his fingers inside of me. It took everything I had to keep from squirming. The waitress would stop by every once in a while and that gave me a break. It didn't take long and we were out of there. Having four hands on you and two dicks inside of you is one of the most erotic things. I sucked Troy and Robert was licking my clit. I don't know how many orgasms I had, I lost count. When I woke this morning we were all curled up on the floor together, me in the middle between them. What a strange sensation. I am really afraid to see where this is going to head!

May 14th

I don't know what to think! The ugly green monster is rearing its ugly head and it's not pretty. I haven't seen Troy since Sunday and I'm not sure what is up Robert's ass but I wish it would crawl out. He's been acting like a fucking whiney little girl all week. It's driving me bat shit!

May 15th

Over breakfast this morning I finally got it out of Robert what was up his ass and it was just as I suspected. He's freaking out, thinking that Troy has been contacting me all week while he's at work. Well for fuck's sake they work together, he ought to know. We are going to meet with Troy over at the Big Sports Pub over at the ET center for a beer so that we can both assure the little baby that there is nothing going on. I should have known this wasn't going to be a good idea. I knew deep in my heart this was a bad, bad idea! I never, NEVER, should have let Robert talk me into this silly sex game. Sure it was super erotic. Sure we pushed our sexual limits, but at what cost? Robert and his brilliant fucking ideas.

Now I have to coddle him and hold his hand like the little boy he is acting like. What a mind fuck!

May 16th

I am so tired I can't see straight. Troy and I had to sit there and explain over and over that we weren't meeting in secret, that we weren't exchanging phone calls. You know what - this is all his fault for even suggesting such a crazy damn idea. I should have known that when Robert agreed to let me be a private exotic dancer, and then fucking told his damn ex-wife about it, this whole thing was going to blow up. And blow up it HAS! We finally got him convinced (I think) but he's still acting so damn petulant!

May 24th

Everything has gotten out of control! Robert is acting freaky about everything! I have been working and making more than enough money to support us both. Because of his child support issues and him not helping I am tense. I am taking jobs I don't want to. I'm drinking entirely too much. I nearly wrecked my fucking car last night on the way to a job and he just keeps getting more and more clingy and needy. Every time my pager goes off and I know it's TZRS calling I can't stand it. The calls are coming more and more often. Stupid fucking Jim and Terry put a damn web page out and I keep getting calls at all hours of the night. The money is good but the calls are getting later and later. I can't do this much longer!

May 27th

I finally broke down and called my mom. I didn't tell her exactly to what extent things were going on between Robert and me but I explained to her that I had been working as an exotic dancer since I left home in February. I didn't tell her about the sex.

She's a smart woman and I think she put it together. She may not know about a lot of things but I know she figured it out when I broke down and fell apart. I told her things have gone bad with Robert and I cried and couldn't stop. I didn't want to admit to my mother the shame I felt but she knew there was NO WAY we could be surviving in Boise with Robert's situation. I never really had to say a word to my mom about the sex, she just blew it off. Well the shit hit the fan when her buddy Gordie, who brought her to my house, a mother fucker I can't stand and she knows it, took us to dinner. He called me a bitch at the club we were at for dinner and drinks, and I punched him and knocked him out of the booth and he got thrown out. We didn't know where he had gone and frankly I didn't care. Anyway this can't last much longer.

July 3rd

It's over! Over over over. The apartment, the exotic dancer life, the whole 9 yards. Robert and I went to the festival to try to recover from everything that started in January and it's finished. I quit the job with TZRS and we haven't had the influx of money because he was relying far too much on me being a whore. I took a modicum income job because I can't stand being with a different person all the time. We had a huge sad blow out last night and the furniture is destroyed all over the bedroom, including my most prized armoire. It is busted into a million pieces. His clothes are scattered all over the lawn. I'm looking out of the big picture window and watching him pick up his fucking clothes that I threw out there, exactly where he and his shit fucking belongs!

Author's Note:

This was a while ago…no, things are not better. Yes Robert is gone, but sadly I am still hurting. Yes, I love sex, but really? At what cost? I loved the threesome. It was one of the most erotic things I have experienced. However, the pain physically doesn't compare to the loss of relationships. If you have never had a threesome it is hard to explain how it feels. If you have, then you know the damage it can do at the end of the day. The erotic sensations don't override the damage after all is done and said.

Excerpt Fourteen

Author's Introduction:

It was 1994 and I was experiencing my own little earth shaking spiritual revival. I've always been "religious" and over the top when it comes to believing the Bible but this was different. I was eating, drinking and breathing the word of God and seeing some amazing things happen.

Then one night when I was in prayer and reading scriptures it occurred to me that I needed to share my story with the world. I felt like God was getting me fired up to speak. I was so excited about it I placed an ad in a Christian magazine called Charisma. In the ad, I offered to be a speaker and tell others how God changed my life.

As it turns out, prisons allow the inmates to read spiritual material and Charisma is a Christian magazine, so I began to hear from inmates across the country asking me to come speak. I never ever dreamt inmates would be my audience. (LOL)

After my ad came out in print I got really scared! I was full of self-doubt and told myself, "You have no clue what you are doing! You will embarrass yourself and wind up looking like a stupid fool."

In the days to follow I received a few phone calls off the ad inviting me to speak at a few conferences. I was also featured in a prison magazine and received a call from the Geraldo Rivera show to come speak. That really scared me! I bowed out by saying I was completely booked up. By then I just wanted to forget the whole dumb idea! There was no way in hell I was going to get in front of a bunch of strangers and risk being humiliated.

I still had the fear from my past. The home I grew up in as a child had been filled with domestic violence where my parents spent a great deal of time fighting and my father spoke often of killing us and then committing suicide himself.

I was terrified at the thought of exposing those secrets, showing vulnerability and letting my guard down in front of people. I let that fear get a grip on me and it stopped me from pursuing my passion!

When I received letters from inmates, I would write back to them to share my life changing experience with them. One inmate named Charlie Hawkins made a particularly big impression on me. These are LETTERS FROM CHARLIE.

03.22.1994

Hello Laura, how are things with you at this time, fine hopefully. I got your address off an ad I saw in the Charisma Magazine.

Now Laura, I'm a black man on death row. I mean no disrespect writing to you and you have nothing to fear. I have many stories I'd like to tell you. Let me start by saying that I'm in prison for robbery and murder. It's my own crazy mistakes that I have been paying for the last twenty eight years of my life.

My birthday is April 10, 1940 and I was born in the state of Georgia.

Charlie

04.04.1994

Miss Laura, I was born on a big plantation in Georgia. My grandmother was a missionary, school teacher and midwife. When I was 8 years old we moved into the city and my grandmother died that year. My mother took over as a midwife and I was promoted to be her helper. We had a big 10 room house that we used for the ladies that were giving birth.

My mother would have the ladies come and stay with us when it was their time. I would keep the water hot, fetch clean towels and sometimes hold the ladies hands. It would get very painful and some of the ladies would try to pull the baby out by themselves. I had to keep their hands out of my mother's way. I helped her deliver babies until I was 14 years old.

Now sometimes we would have to go to other people's homes because some of the ladies couldn't make it to our house on time. My mother did not discriminate. She took care of white women who got pregnant by black men.

They had to come to my mother because if they went to the city hospital the doctor would let them bleed to death and let the baby die. Some of the nurses at the hospital knew what was going on so they would take the babies and give them to my mother.

My mother would then give them to the other black women in the neighborhood. The youngest girl that ever came to our house was Peggy. She was 10 years old and pregnant by her father. He raped her and then her mother ran off when she found out about it.

My mother took over and put him put in jail but it did no good, the plantation boss man got him out. He said Peggy was just a 'nigger' and meant nothing. He said he needed his 'nigger' out of jail to work on his land. The law man let her daddy go.

Charlie

04.14.1994

Miss Laura, let me tell you how my downfall began. I was 23 years old and living with 3 young ladies at the time. These ladies were thieves and killed for money.

I went along with it because I wanted to impress them and be accepted. We got away with more than fifty robberies and at least five murders. Then a buddy of mine turned me in and I received two death sentences, two life sentences and one twenty two year sentence.

My grandmother's name was Mattie Green. She was born into slavery in 1860. Mattie began at the age of nine to be a nurse maid to the plantation owner's daughter. Her name was Elizabeth and she was nine years older than Mattie.

She was off to the young ladies school at the age of eighteen and she took Mattie with her. They lived together and at night Elizabeth would teach Mattie how to read and write. They both decided to join up with some missionaries that went from country to country.

Then after eight years of being with the missionaries they returned home because they couldn't watch the suffering any longer. Every country they went into the people were starving and dying from disease.

The soldiers were raping men, women and children and then cutting their throats. They saw bellies cut open, dresses lifted up around the thighs and sperm running out of the vagina and anus. The buzzards were after the bodies like mad. The soldiers walked around with big smiles on their faces.

When Mattie and Elizabeth got back home Elizabeth made her father build Mattie a big church on the plantation for the blacks. Mattie and her mother, LuLu, lived in a one roomed cabin on the plantation. Mattie's mother worked for "Liz's" mother and after LuLu died Mattie had the cabin all to herself.

One night Mattie was taking her bath and getting ready for bed. The cabin had a few cracks in the walls that allowed someone to look in. Along came two young black men that lived on the plantation. They were coming back from the moonshine still that they owned in the forest.

They had been drinking and decided to peek through the cracks of the cabin. They saw Mattie's naked body and, unable to turn off their desires, they kicked the door in and raped Mattie. She put up a fight but lost. After both of them had finished with her they left without saying a word. She kept quiet about the rape until she could no longer conceal her pregnancy.

One day she got both those men into her church. One was named Frank Morgan and the other Charlie Taylor. She began to undress and they thought she was going crazy. When they saw her swollen belly they didn't say a word. She asked, "Now which one of you is this baby's father?

Neither could say a word. Mattie said, "Both of you will have to take care of this baby."

They did by selling moonshine, homemade wine, and stealing the boss man's pigs and chickens to give Mattie money for the baby. They even stole a cow, put boots on the cows four feet backwards to confuse the authorities as to which way they went.

When the baby, my mother, was born Mattie asked both of them to name her. It was decided she would be called Rose. Mattie taught Rose everything she knew, then at the age of twenty three Rose ran off with a soldier by the name of Johnny Hawkins, my father. They got married but Johnny went off to war and never came back.

Charlie

04.21.1994

Miss Laura, We had these door-to-door salesmen in our neighborhood when I was a kid. One day I watched a salesman take some dresses into Mrs. Emma Cox's house.

They were very pretty dresses so I decided to check it out. I went around the house and peeked in through the side door. I saw Mrs. Emma lying back on the bed with her dress up around her hips. The salesman was standing between her legs and slapping her face.

She had both of her hands over her face. He stopped hitting her and pulled his pants down. He was sticking out in front. He lifted both her legs in the air and pushed them back. Then he threw himself on top of her and started moving his body up and down.

Mrs. Emma still had her face covered when he stopped moving. He straightened up and cleaned himself off with the bed sheet. Then he pulled up his pants and went back to slapping her face again.

When he was finished he took the dresses and walked out without looking back. She just laid there with her legs wide open for about five minutes. Then she got up and took the sheet off the bed and went into the kitchen crying.

We also had "gypsy" salesmen that were low down, dirty and nasty. They usually ran in pairs so that one could rape the women and the other could steal things from the house. They would force the women to get on their hands and knees and then they would rape them from behind.

Mrs. Alice Williams put up a fight and won. She stuck her fingers in the insurance man's eyes and while he was hollering for help she was beating him with the fire iron. The sheriff put her in jail by saying she was crazy, then from jail she went to the state crazy house.

The sheriff didn't do anything to the insurance man because the sheriff was doing the same thing to the ladies himself. Only difference was, the sheriff did it to the younger girls. He would catch them going home from working at the rich white ladies homes. He would pick them up and tell them that they had an arrest warrant out for them from Mrs. Smith who claimed they had taken money from her purse.

He would tell the girls, "I'm sure we can work this out so don't you worry." Then he would get into their panties before letting them go.

Now my mother, Rose, didn't trust anyone. If there was a knock on the front door she would sneak out back and circle around the house to see who it was. She kept an ice pick in her bra and told me if I ever saw her fighting with a man to get the fire iron and beat his head with it.

It was 1948-1949 and women were working at saw mills, dipping turpentine, loading pulp wood, and unloading 200 pound sacks of fertilizer. They would lug the fertilizer across the fields in five gallon buckets to the planters that were planting corn, cotton, peanuts and some of those women were pregnant and carrying babies on their backs.

They had to because the husband had run off because of his shame or had been hung for trying to speak up for his loved ones. All of the blacks in the southern states were Baptist.

Charlie

05.11.1994

Hello Laura, how are you? I'm doing fine myself. According to my mother, Rose, Mattie had great spiritual powers. She healed a lot of people with her special herbs, the ones she mixed together with special plants.

Rose says she healed everything but cancer, blindness and bone disease. Those were the only diseases she couldn't heal with her powers. Then Mattie lost all her powers after she got raped. It lasted seven years and then she was back at her work healing people's sickness.

Mattie's body went through some funny changes after she had her baby. She would lie in bed and cry about how bad her body was hurting for sexual release. But Mattie refused to accept a man to enter into her body sexually.

Rose said Mattie would release herself sexually without using her hands on her body. This went on for seven years and then it stopped just like that. Laura, send me your shoe size, hat size and sweater size. I will make you something pretty.

I will show you what I do with some of my time in this place. My job at this prison is working at the garment factory where they make all the inmates clothes. God bless you.

Charlie

05.12.1994

Hello Laura, how are things with you? While I'm thinking about it I want to tell you about this lady, Lisa. I'm in prison for killing her father. She is a telephone operator for the big phone company in this state.

Lisa never knew her mother. Her mother ran off with another man two weeks after she was born. That left her father to raise her. At age 13 her father began to use his tongue on her young body, only his tongue and fingers.

He began to penetrate her at age 16. That was the year I came along and messed things up in her life by killing her father. For twenty eight years now I have been getting 4 hate letters a year from Lisa.

She starts all of her letters off by asking, "When are you coming home to me? I miss you so much. My body needs you so bad. I'm hurting inside for your love. Please hurry I need you so bad. "Why don't you make a run for it?" You know I will pick you up. I'm getting old and I want to make a baby with you."

"Here is some money and a picture of me to keep you going until my next letter." The money will be the same every time, one hundred dollars. All the pictures would be "sexy" pictures. She would be dressed in different sexy outfits standing in front of her mirror.

Now I could keep the money and pictures, but I don't. I send both back always. She will cry about it and send it to me again. Crying and cussing me out. "What have they done to you up there? Have they made a "fagget" out of you? You don't like beautiful ladies anymore?"

"You better not let that happen to you. I don't want my baby to be a sissy and why did you send the money back? I want you to have it for yourself." She is living by herself and not messing around with other men.

She wrote me once telling me how she hates me because I killed her first love. She is a beautiful woman. She sent me one real sexy picture where she had on a short red dress and high heels. She was getting out of her car with a smile on her face and her legs were open so I could see her panties.

She was real mad when I sent the picture back to her. She said, "Don't you know I paid a hooker fifty dollars to take my picture and you sent it back like a fool." She really goes off when Christmas comes around. All of her letters end the same way, "I hate you for destroying my body like you did."

Now I want to tell you about Rose, my mother. She would never let me take a bath by myself or sleep alone. She would talk crazy about my body when she was giving me my bath. Stuff like, "It is growing in my hand. It is long enough but not fat enough. It has to grow some more before it will be ready for me."

"Then it will be ready to make my Johnny-Frank for me." She would oil it and play with it. In bed she would make me kiss and lick her whole body. This went on until I was twelve years old. It started when I was eight. I did not penetrate her until I was twelve.

Our next door neighbor was named Emma. She was a beautician. She had her own beauty parlor and Rose was jealous of her. Emma was twenty five years old, 6' and about 160 pounds with yellow skin tone and she was very pretty.

Rose could not stand to look at Emma. I would sneak out and cut wood and clean Emma's yard whenever I got the chance. I liked her. She would buy me things. Rose had it in her head that Emma was evil and that she was a red headed devil.

Rose had it in her head that Emma was out to get me and take me away from her. She said Emma would make me sick for her body by saving up all her dirty rags from her monthly period and boil all of the blood out of them.

Then she would take the nasty water and make soup out of it and feed me the soup. Rose said it worked. I would never have a taste for no other ladies and that all of the women in the town did this to their men.

One day Rose came looking for me. She must have known I was at Emma's house because she slipped into the house and caught me sitting in Emma's lap. I was licking the inside of Emma's mouth out. Emma loved that!

They had a big fight and Rose told her to stay away from me or she would kill her. I stayed away from Emma for a few weeks. Then one day she caught me at the store buying sugar and eggs for Rose.

She told me she really missed my sweet kisses and she wanted me to wait until dark when Rose went to sleep and slip into her house. She would leave her side door open for me to come in but make sure Rose is asleep.

At first I was afraid to do it but I got to thinking about how good she smelled and how pretty she was. I made up my mind to try it. When I made sure Rose was asleep I went to Emma. She was naked sitting in the dark waiting for me.

She took me into her lap and began kissing my face and putting her nipples into my mouth. I was twelve years old at the time. She told me to undress myself. She had a mattress on the floor so she lay down and waited for me.

When I got down there with her she took my face in both her hands and told me don't be afraid of nothing I tell you to do. She lay with her back to me and told me to start at the back of her knees and kiss my way up to her butt.

Very slow and easy, up and down each of her thighs. I did like she said and the only thing she would say was, "You is getting good." She began to say crazy things. Things I had never heard before. When I got to her neck she turned over and had me start at her forehead.

She had me kiss and lick my way back down to her knees. Then she stopped me and said, "Now you listen to me and do as I say. She opened her legs and said, "I want you to get at my goodies with your tongue and lips."

Then she said, "Take and kiss it all over with your lips, not your tongue. Make your tongue stiff and poke it into the inside of my thighs and all around, not the inside yet. Just the outside, you are doing it right."

"Just keep poking me with it." Then she stopped me, she had one hand over her goodies. She said, "I want you to just take your tongue and lick only between my two fingers, up and down, slow and easy."

She started moaning and crying and hitting me in the back. Then she stopped moving and said, "Let us clean ourselves up so you can go back home without waking Rose up." We went into the kitchen and she put some water, alcohol and turpentine into a cup.

She had me wash my mouth out good and clean my face and upper body. She kissed me goodnight and I got back into the house without waking Rose. Two nights later I went back for more because she was so exciting.

This time she says to me, "We gonna do something new. I want you to use your knife on me. I want you to stick me with it." Well, I didn't have a knife and I thought she was talking crazy but she said, "The long one that you have between your legs."

She had me start off by kissing her face, licking her nipples and rubbing my hand between her legs. Then she said, "I want you to get between my legs and when I place your knife in my goodies, I want you to push in and out."

She said, "Now I want you to make direct contact with my "button." She put both her legs up on my shoulders and placed my knife into her goodies. Then she told me to speed up and then she started yelling, "stick me deeper!"

Then I began to have chills all over my body and I was feeling real good. She kept me coming back for more. Rose never did catch us but she began to work on me like Emma. After that Rose had to have it every morning before she got up to cook for the house.

Rose got pregnant with my baby. When I turned fourteen I ran away from home.

Charlie

06.09.1994

Hello Laura. I pray that this letter finds you in good health. When I first entered this prison on May 13, 1966 I had a hard time understanding how things worked. There was this guy who was up tight on prison violations.

He had been talking too loud to his next door cell mate so they gave him 30 days in the hole for the offense but first he had to go through a special punishment. They took away all his clothes and left him with nothing but his shoes.

Then they handcuffed the guy to the bars and sprayed him down with cold water. Then they threw salt on his body while he was still wet. He would beg for death because the salt was eating his body. After that they put him on soup and water for twenty seven days.

When he came out of the hole his head was messed up. He would scream and yell, "Would somebody please write my mother and tell her I'm in a world of trouble." We all called him "Benny Bo Lightening" because that was the only name he would answer to.

He was so crazy he took a razor blade and cut both of his balls off and his penis and threw them into the toilet and flushed it. He said, "I have no use for them anyway." The guard beat his head and kicked his ribs in. It was sickness.

We also have these college students come in here, the ones that is studying to be doctors. The state allows them to experiment on those crazy sick guys by giving them different kinds of pills to take and they pay the guys $18 dollars a week.

All of the pills that they take make them so fat some of them can't walk right and can't do nothing but sleep the entire day. Mind control drugs. And the guys that are in prison for rape, they would castrate them and you could see them rubbing their hands between their legs and see blood stains on their pants.

And some of the men here rape other men daily and turn them into sex slaves. They use celebrity names like Elizabeth Taylor, Lena Horne, Diana Ross and Jayne Mansfield. They will dress themselves in ladies outfits to make their lovers jealous of them.

They sell their bodies for cigarettes, dope, five, ten and twenty dollars. The real young ones can get as much as one hundred dollars. They rob and steal from anyone who has anything. They go down to the chapel and tell the preacher that they in love and they want to get married.

Charlie

07.15.1994

Hello Laura, how are things with you? I was transferred to another prison last month. The new place is about three hundred miles south of the old prison. It sits on an air force base and we live in big block rooms that hold about sixty five men.

There are about one thousand men living here. The place is nice and one hundred times better than the old prison that I left behind. We even have telephones here and can make calls anytime we want to but no one can call us.

The guards are not mean and they have a lot of respect for the women who work here. It's like a big school with lots of land and room to move around in. There are lots of big trees and wild animals here. "My luck has changed" and for the first time in my life I am really happy!

Charlie

Author's Note:

Charlie's letters dwindled over the years and then they stopped altogether. In January of 2002 I received a letter from an official at the Florida State prison informing me that Charlie was dead. It saddened me to know that I'd never hear from my old friend again but I was glad that he had found happiness and was at peace in the end.

Excerpt Fifteen

Author's Note:

These are journal entries that I wrote venting about my husband, Mike. We had blended our families together, him with his 2 kids, Amy & Derek, and me with my one, Roxy. I thought my role in this stage of my life was to be a stay at home mom. I took in his kids full time thinking we'd be one big happy family. Soon after my husband & I married, he lost his job; he was forced to travel for work more and more. His ex-wife, Tina, started working more in the evenings too so I had their kids more than either one of them. Things started to get rough as his kids were becoming teens and I was in the middle of another custody battle for my own daughter.

June 9th

Well shit has hit the fan! I cannot believe all that is happening. I was at Renae's and got a bad sickening feeling. I told her I needed to go home and check on the kids. When I arrived Derek was laying on the couch acting strange. He was under a blanket and I asked why since it was so hot out and we aren't even running the air conditioner yet. He said he was cold and tired. I said ok but something in my gut told me I needed to stay nearby. I sat in my office and couldn't even work. I turned and asked him if everything was okay. He looked very upset but he said yes. I got worried for reasons I didn't know yet. I couldn't move and felt I needed to stay right there with him. I asked several times if he needed anything and told him that he could talk to me if he wanted and that I was there for him. He didn't really respond and kinda brushed me off. I could sense something was wrong. An hour later the doorbell rang. I had to get up to go get the door. It was his mom. She said she needed to take him home to talk to him. I could hear Derek grumbling and getting up. She told him as he walked by to hurry up and come on. I told her he was acting strange and wondered why she wasn't at work and she said she needed to talk to him. After she got him out the door he demanded her to come on and she snapped and said to go get in the car while we talk. He turned and walked slowly to her car and she said can I ask you something? I said, "yeah." She stepped inside and shut the door. Quietly she asked if we had ever been missing any money around the house. I kinda laughed and hesitated to answer. A million thoughts raced through my mind. So since I haven't written for a while I need to back up a minute…

For the last year, or at least since the end of last summer, things with me and the kids have been getting very difficult. I try to teach them real world things like how to clean, working on how to cook, finances, manners and behavior. It's been very difficult and I wonder if I will have any effect on them this late in their childhood. But I feel like I have them the majority of their waking hours so I need to do something to prepare them for life. I really don't feel like I would do them any favors to act like a sitter and let them do as they please. And I don't get paid to be a sitter or their maid. Anyways I have lost my cool a lot! I get very tired of them all fighting, their attitudes and also Mike's kids trying to boss my daughter around even when I am in the room. I tell them I am the parent and it's not their responsibility to worry about her. I have been very nice about it but I don't understand why they feel the need to "parent" her. I had issues also with Derek telling lies, avoiding the truth, & basically being a smart ass.

Also I went through sickness for months last year - then had surgery last summer. All this time I had Mike's kids. Never did I have a break or help when I was sick since he was gone for work.

Their mom continued to work until 9pm and several times I would find out she had taken the day off but I still had her kids! Even after my surgery I didn't have anyone to help. My mom was out of town for work too. My dad took me to the doctor and back home and that was it. He didn't stay but called to check in a time or two.

I had Mike's kids to look after while I recovered. They came in a few hours after I had gotten home and asked me what was for dinner. I cried and cried and had never felt so used and alone. Then a few weeks after recovery we found out my Grandmother was dying of cancer. She was in the final stages when the doctors discovered it. So we moved her to mom's house and I helped take care of her during her last few weeks. I still took care of the kids too. Tina did occasionally find someone else to take them to some of their sports activities while I took care of my grandmother. After her funeral I was put right back into taking care of all the kids full time alone; everyone expected me to pick the slack back up and do it all again. Plus when I was getting packed and telling the kids they would miss a day of school for the funeral, Amy got very angry with me and asked why the hell she needed to go since it wasn't even her family. That still feels like a stab to the gut! I decided I didn't want her to go. My entire family has been so accepting of Mike and his kids and they all treat his kids like they are mine and part of our family. So I just can't believe she would say such a thing. She was so dead serious too. Mike's mom talked to her and asked her to think about if her grandma died, how would she feel if I had said the same thing to her? I guess she realized what a brat she had been because she shut up and went with us.

Then at the funeral everyone was talking to her and her brother because they were crying. I was so very hurt that they took away so much from me. Memories people had about my grandmother were shared with my step kids. How unfair it felt and still does. So maybe things were difficult because of my own grief that I was ignoring. I really never got a chance to grieve. I was so busy with the kids right after her death. There was a time with Derek that I asked him to do something and while he did do it, he didn't complete the task fully. I think he said it was cold in the house and I said that the fire went out. So I asked him to put wood on the stove (in the fireplace). So he only stacked wood in the fireplace and didn't start the fire, then went outside to skate. I asked him to come back in and get the fire going and he threw a tantrum. He started throwing wood and yelling at me about how he wasn't going to be my slave. This started happening a lot where he would look at me with this mean look and ignore me OR he would throw a 2 year old tantrum. Several times he would throw things and I started to get a little scared of his temper. His parents didn't believe me and also wouldn't help me discipline. In fact at one point around this time Tina told me to my face in front of the kids that she didn't agree with the need to discipline and that it wouldn't be enforced at her house. Sometimes I would be desperate and tell her to please help me find a solution to the behavioral problems. All she would do is say, "I will talk to him."

So then during all this Derek kept finding money. During the last summer he found several twenty's on the ground in different parking lots when he was with his mom. We couldn't believe his luck to be finding money all over the place. My husband said it must be because he was so short he saw more on the ground than we did. I agreed since my daughter would find coins all the time and put them in her piggy bank; but twenty dollar bills? Then it started to be more, over Christmas he found a hundred dollar bill in the parking lot with his mom. Then soon after it was a couple hundred. Amy started to get mad and wasn't sure how she could miss these things since she said she was walking in front of him. I could tell she was very suspicious.

Around this time I also started to notice things out of place in my bedroom and even in my own clothes dresser. One time Mike and I had been fighting or arguing about the kids and he left for work kind of mad. I noticed later that he had gotten into the money envelope that we had hidden and left it out in the middle of the floor. I put it back where it belonged and thought nothing of it. Then the next week it happened again. I started to wonder what the hell he was spending money on. We had arguments a lot around Christmas because he would buy gifts for the family but address it to me and he would spend a few hundred bucks which I felt was too much. I always felt like I didn't matter because he never bought anything really for me.

Anyways the following few days I found the envelope out in the middle of the floor again and I decided I would confront him about it since by now it was after Christmas. I counted the money and noticed it was very low. We usually kept thousands of dollars in there on hand. We had under two grand left. I was pissed. I thought the only thing he could have spent thousands on must be to retain an attorney for divorce. I really feel that low about our relationship. I asked him over the phone what he was spending the money on and he played dumb so I told him point blank I knew he took thousands out of the envelope over the past while. He said he didn't and actually hadn't taken money out for a while. That got me really paranoid. We both started talking about the last time we had gotten into the envelope to take money out and the last time each of us counted it and what we put in and so forth.

We couldn't figure it out and I had been having problems the previous year with coming home and doors being open. I had the neighbor put a safety stick in our sliding glass door and started double checking the locks all the doors and windows. Mike had even bought me a hand gun the previous Christmas since I was scared when he was gone.

Fast forward again…when the money went missing I got scared. Mike told me to go deposit it immediately. Oh and there was a time just before this happened that I took a $100 bill out to go Christmas shopping since we didn't have any money in our account. I never made it to the store that day and at night when I changed into my pajamas I remembered and put the money in my top drawer for the next day. A week later I remembered that I didn't know where it had gone. I was positive that I put it in my dresser but it wasn't there. I searched the house. Finally out of desperation I told the kids I must have misplaced a $100 bill and needed help finding it. They all (supposedly) hadn't seen it. I wrote it off as my dumb mistake and figured I would find it eventually. It was in the back of my mind as I noticed our cash missing in our envelope. But even my own husband was starting to question my mind.

So anyways Tina asked me if we were missing money and I hesitated but told her yes. I told her about our savings envelope and the times I have been missing money in my business petty cash & customer deposits and the money in my dresser drawer. She was pretty upset about it all. I guess her boyfriend's son was also suspected since they were at her parent's house with them this weekend. Her mom was missing a couple hundred bucks. She asked the boys about it (not sure why she suspected them) and they gave different stories. She was going back to the house to ask her son about things again to try to figure out who took the money. I noticed after they left that a gun case was in the hallway instead of in the closet and remembered that I found it out the other day too. I put it away wondered what the kids were looking for that they would be moving the guns around.

She called later and said yes Derek took the money. He admitted it only after she found part of the money in his snow pants pocket. She wondered if I would search his room here to look for cash. She said to search pockets. I said ok. I didn't find any money though. I didn't go through his room very well though either. I didn't feel it was my place to as the stepmom. She said he admitted that her boyfriend's son stole from the small market by her parent's house and that he was pressuring Derek to do it too but that he didn't. He said that was why he stole the money from his grandma because he wanted to show he could steal too. She said she is still talking to him and finding things out and would keep in touch.

I have a sinking feeling he is on drugs and stealing to support his habit. It would make sense since he has been so angry and lies about everything. Plus he has been talking a lot this past school year about how he was amazed at the drugs people did at school. I was always nervous about those conversations we had but glad he would confide in me or so I thought.

So then tonight when Mike got off work I guess he went straight over to Tina's to see what all was going on and talk to Derek a bit. I was a little upset because he hadn't talked to me about it right away. He got home and we were eating dinner, almost done. He ate a little then he didn't talk about it but I was anxious to know what new news he might have learned. A little while later Amy was getting ready to go to her mom's and Mike took her outside to talk to her. I guessed he was telling her what was happening and he still hadn't talked to me so I was wondering if I was going to have to wait until bedtime. They talked out there for a long time, before she left for her mom's.

Later after Roxy was in bed, Mike finally told me more. Basically Derek admitted that he stole the money from his grandma and that he also stole a few hundred from us but he wouldn't give reasons why or what he spent the money on. He doesn't have anything new or unusual that he would have bought. Mike said that Derek told them too that he was going to kill himself and had gotten a gun out of the hall closet to do it. I realized then that is when I came home. I think the gun was under the blanket. I must have stopped him from doing it. He didn't really give any reasons to why he would kill himself but Mike said they have to take that very seriously so we are clearing the house of all guns and medications. He said that Derek will have to be on 24 hour watch. I agreed but asked how I was to do that and he said well I understand you can't always be with him but do your best to not let him be alone.

Neither one of us slept well and luckily Tina took another day off work so I wouldn't have to deal with the situation alone. More came out today as Tina started finding pawn slips and strange things in her house. No details just that he admitted to more money he stole – from her boyfriend, from us, and others. I am starting to think there is a lot more to this since he isn't being completely truthful with anyone.

Tina ended up taking the whole week off work. More information came out daily. This has been really rough on us all. One night she was supposed to come by to talk to us without the kids about what we would do but she didn't come when she was supposed to. Mike called and she was trying to avoid it. She always flakes out so eventually she said fine she would come over.

She ended up bringing Derek and asking him a bunch more questions about why he did it. I was mad because I needed a game plan about what we would do. I was pissed because supposedly he didn't feel loved. But OUR household revolves around him! When Tina questioned him she would ask leading questions instead of making him answer. For example: 'Derek did you do this because your dad and I are divorced?' OR 'Derek did you do this because your dad works a lot?' OR 'Derek did you do this because I don't spend enough time with you?' Etc! What the hell? I am so pissed this was happening.

At one point Tina told Derek to go inside and call Mike's parents to tell them he stole money from them and apologize. When he did I confronted Tina and Mike about what they were doing. I told them I was pissed they are letting Derek use excuses for his behavior. I also was pissed because they think that Derek is doing this because he is jealous of the time his dad and I spend together. WE DON'T GET ANY TIME ALONE TOGETHER!!!!! I just about screamed it! I am so fucking angry. How dare he try to use such a bull shit lie of an excuse!

He came back out after being on the phone and Tina asked if he apologized and he hesitated and she got pissed. She said you don't even feel sorry for what you did! Then he said oh I did say I was sorry. She asked how the conversation went but you could tell he was bull shitting! She knew it too and asked what the hell was wrong with him. She said she is having a hard time finding a counselor with an appointment this week. Mike told her to keep trying. She said she is on a couple of waiting lists. She also said that he will start working off the money he stole from her parents next week. So I won't have to watch him.

Earlier in the week I finally searched Derek's room. Tina kept asking us to do it and Mike wouldn't so I finally said fuck it I will. I tore the place a part. Didn't find anything drug related but asked Tina if she thought Derek was on drugs. She cried and said she cannot imagine him doing that. I said well I couldn't imagine him stealing so much either. She said I know I know the signs point to it. I did find in his room some drawings and notes under the mattress. They were statements and drawings about death, killing and wanting to die or leave and run away. I found some things that looked like he was trying to make a bomb out of fireworks but Mike said all boys do things like that.

July 3rd

So now several weeks have passed and things haven't gotten much better. Derek has been staying at his grandparent's house working. We have discovered more money that had been stolen. Mike and I know it to be thousands of dollars gone. Plus I can remember times he disappeared at my friends' houses and I would catch him in bedrooms and tell him he isn't allowed to do that. I don't know why I didn't think much of it at the time. Also I have some friends that were missing cash but can't confirm if it was around the time we visited.

The latest is that Tina has found Derek's notes of threats to run away. Also she found a large knife in his backpack. The suicide threat has been forgotten by his parents so no one has been watching him all the time. He is allowed to go off on his own at times at his grandparents. The biggest thing going on right now is fucking Tina is saying that she won't allow Mike to visit Derek anymore because he is a bad father. I feel this is all lies and Derek is just trying to push the blame onto someone else and Tina is buying it.

Mike had been over at her parents' house talking to the family and hanging out and it wasn't until he was ready to take the kids to his parent's house that Tina pulled him aside to tell him his son didn't want to go with him and she wouldn't make him. She said that she felt it was best if he didn't have visitation for a while. When I found out I was pissed!!!! She hasn't even been taking him to his counseling appointments. She found the notes and the knife and she did nothing about it! What a great fucking mom. I have nothing nice to say about her anymore. Mike is beside himself depressed! I have never seen him so upset and I thought he wasn't doing well a few weeks ago when this started. He has hit a new low and I don't blame him at all. I think we need to get courts involved asap! Mike has every right to his children and she cannot stop his visitation! It sucks it's a holiday right now!

July 22nd

I found drugs!!! I don't know what to do. I need to get this off my chest and sort things out. Mike just took the kids out to pick up clothes at their moms. We had just picked up Derek from his grandparents to bring him home for the weekend and he was acting weird the whole time about his backpack. He wouldn't leave it alone! I was kinda mad that he is allowed to have 2 friends spending the night tonight too! He should be grounded for life! It's like he got away with stealing and lying!!!! There hasn't been a punishment yet! Anyways I was walking past his room and felt weird like I hit a brick wall. I had a strange feeling that I needed to look in his backpack. As wrong as it is, I did it because of this overwhelming feeling I had. Well I found pot and papers in 2 different pockets! I took it out and hid it under my bed for now. I don't know how to tell Mike. I don't know if he will leave me for going through his son's stuff. But I can't explain why I did either. Of course his son went through my room all the time for a year! Dang I don't know what I will do. It is late (10 pm) and I won't be able to sleep but how do I tell Mike! I don't know. I am freaking out!!!

August 18th

It really bothers me that I cannot plan with Mike and Tina's custody schedule or lack thereof I should say. Mike doesn't think it should be an issue and that I should tell everyone if I have plans so that they know. But why can't they tell me if they are changing the schedule. It affects my household and my plans if the kids' plans are constantly changing. Sports are starting up soon too. I need a heads up for games. Honestly I don't want to go if Tina is there. I am trying to be civil and also support the kids but if she refuses to deal with me, I just want to avoid her too.

If I don't allow kids to be here when Mike's not here, how is that going to affect our relationship and my relationship with the kids? Am I right to take Derek's house key away? Also if he goes to the school in his mom's district/boundaries then he won't be close to my house to just walk home after school or after the bus. Do I really now have to go out of my way to pick him up from there? Actually it won't work! I have my own daughter to pick up from school now. I wish someone would communicate things with me. I have no clue how things are going to go when school starts next week. It's already bad enough that now all of our 3 kids are at different schools! I assume Amy will start driving herself to school which is another sore subject – no discussion on who will pay for gas, repairs etc. If her mom is giving her the car and there wasn't discussion with us about it at all, she should have to pay for everything to go along with it.

Money issues with Tina are really bugging me. Am I being controlling by wanting Mike to ask her for money? She should have to pay half of Derek's boot camp bill and the thing is she agreed to pay half of it. $15,000 is a lot of money to swallow but I did. I didn't question Mike's decision to spend it sending Derek away. And I heard with my own ears that Tina would help out with the bills. He said that if she never pays he will tell her to just pay for all the kids' extra costs without his help until they are both 18, but I don't trust he will communicate that either. I don't trust her to ever pay a dime. We pay her child support yet we have paid for almost every activity for the last few years. Mostly because she isn't here when they ask for the money or school expenses. When it was just me, I started asking the kids to wait until their mom got home and ask her for the money they needed. And still at the last minute I would end up giving them a check for what they needed.

Do I have the right to ask him to consult with me before spending money on his kids? I always ask before spending our money on Roxy.

September 8th

I was sleeping in on Sunday morning and I heard the door being unlocked and opened. I heard Derek come into my house, when he thought I should be gone at church and knowingly while Mike was out of town. I jumped out of bed and ran down the hall to find him there. He asked rudely, "What are you doing here?" To which I replied, "This is my house. What are you doing here?" He said, "Getting stuff." I reminded him that he wasn't allowed to come over and be in the house alone. He responded in his smart ass tone, "Well you are here." I told him he didn't know that before he came over and let himself in. And he didn't know before he let himself into the house since my car was in the garage.

Next he started blaming his mom saying his mom told him to come over. I told him his mom is also aware of the rules and that next time he needs to call and make sure I am home. He continued denying responsibility and said that his mom told him he could come over. I told him that his mom doesn't live here and the rule here is that he needs to make sure someone is home before he comes over.

At that point I realized he had his druggie friend here with him. He was hiding in Derek's room! This is the 'friend' who was doing drugs with him at school. I was really pissed then! We all agreed at boot camp that he was no longer allowed to hang out with the old friends whom he did drugs with. Derek did a huge loud exhale and turned and walked into the garage. I followed behind and he came back in with tools and said he was taking the wheels off his skateboard. I told him to make sure they were put back in place and he said like a smart ass that he always does. I had to walk away. I was so done arguing with him and couldn't believe he was here. I knew I would lose all control if I sat there watching and waiting for them to leave. I stayed nearby on the couch. They stayed in the room and he left a little bit later without saying anything and in somewhat of a hurry. When I walked by his room to close the door the tools were still on the bed. This crosses my line and I don't know who to be pissed at. Derek, his mother (if what he said was true - of course his mother had to have allowed him to be hanging out with the old friend) or/and Mike. It feels like they all don't give one shit about me and the fact that this is my house too.

I am lost, completely lost. I feel like my identity is lost. I feel depressed. I miss the kids. Even though Amy is still here I can't help but feel like she is lost too. She doesn't connect with me like she used to. She called yesterday to say she was playing in the varsity game and I said "yeah that's ok, that's so cool" and she snaps and says she wasn't "asking permission! I am going to play." I said, "I know I think that is awesome that they want you to play." She says she gets to be goalie and I say, "Oh gosh I wish I would have gone to the game to see it and I hope you don't get too many bruises." She is snappy and says she "wants bruises." I kind of laugh it off and tell her to have fun and that I love her.

I wanted to go to the game but Roxy has activities too sometimes. I can't do it all anymore. I have done that and worn myself out and in the end only your kids benefit. Not me, not my daughter. But I don't understand why Amy is so short with me. Maybe I am doing something wrong. I wish I knew so I could correct it. I feel like I am just an intruder into their lives. I felt like she didn't want to have to call me to tell me. It's not the first time I have gotten that impression. If she doesn't want to hang out over here then she shouldn't have to call and check in with me. But if I am responsible for her since she is here, then it should probably be necessary for me to know where she is. It is about respect. I should know where the kids are that I am responsible for in my own house. I really don't think I am too far out of line here. And maybe she is just being a typical teen too. I just don't know because I don't remember her acting this way before life as we knew it fell apart a few months ago.

September 30th

The worst part of it all is feeling so alone, so utterly alone; no one to understand or even listen. I keep thinking that maybe if I talk about it with friends, or family even, sometimes again and again, someone-somewhere will get it and listen and help me. But it doesn't happen. Maybe the solution is within me but right now the pain is so great it is hard to see any light at the end of the tunnel. I am starting to feel like even the Lord has abandoned me. Why can I not feel peace or happiness? Why can I not find the solution to this complex puzzle? Why is He not helping me?

If Derek was my own son I know this would have been somewhat resolved by now. It is so hard knowing that what you feel is best and how you should handle it cannot be done since you are not the biological parent. Even though you had him more than any other parent it doesn't matter what you think or how you feel about it. I do want him here so badly. I miss being his buddy and helping him out and taking him places. I miss it badly. But when he knows I have no say in what he does, that is when things go bad. He was reaching out for me to help him but legally I couldn't. I was yelling for his parents to help him but no one would listen and no one heard. His school was calling and knew something was up but still his parents refused to see what was going on. I don't know what else I could have possibly done. How can I turn back and take him back in; after such betrayal and him having no remorse and refusing to have any discussion about it. He stole not just money and things but he stole my sense of security and trust in a family where I didn't fully know my place anyways. Now I really feel out of place as his mom trashes my name; my husband thinks I am a bitch and maybe going crazy; my step kids have no respect for me or my rules, my morals, values, beliefs; and the worst is that no one respects my role & my boundaries in my own home. According to Mike, I can't just change the lock and lock them all out when he is not home. I can't have peace and quiet and I can't just plan on no company because one of them "may need something from my home." And no one has the respect to call and make sure it's a good time to come over. I regret not putting boundaries in place when I got here. I regret it even though I know I had no problem with it back then. I still should have set up my personal boundaries and taught them to respect me before things got so out of hand.

Maybe Derek is doing better, although I hear and see otherwise. I think he is getting better at hiding or avoiding his feelings. I am stuck at the time when this all went down - when he sat in my living room and argued with Mike about everything. He denied seeing any problems with his actions, his lying, manipulating, stealing, drugs, smoking, and all his bad behavior. His anger and hatred towards life and us was just frightening. Yes he did go to boot camp and seemed to have done well. However comments started before we left. He was angry we sent him there. Why the hell did he have to be there? He didn't see any problem with smoking dope. He didn't see any problem with his attire, hair or jewelry. He didn't see any reason why he was sent there and we weren't sent to a camp to deal with our issues. I agree with the last one. We never did get any help or discuss what led up to this – our responsibility for his behavior. I felt like I was holding the load for years. Going to teacher conferences, school functions, volunteering, sports activities, running them everywhere, cooking for them and feeding them, taking care of them when they were sick, trying to find solutions to problems in the home; and dealing with the 2 biological parents who refused to take responsibility for their children. I was alone in discipline and never backed up when trying to discuss a situation that needed to be addressed. I was told it was my problem only at my house and also that rules and/or consequences at my house will not be enforced at the other or just an "I'll talk to them about it" but never, NEVER were there any consequences for any wrong doings. Unless I enforced one, however even my own spouse wouldn't back me up on that either.

Mike is always gone so he wouldn't know what was going on or how could he possibly do anything being so far away. Then when he did come home he refused to try to communicate with me or figure out what had been going on before taking over, so all rules and consequences went out the door when he came in. The kids aren't dumb either and they knew and still know how it is. They play the system the way kids do.

And I still feel maybe we haven't even hit the target about what really happened. Derek's outbursts and tantrums don't match up with pot. Unless he just has that much anger??? The amount of money he stole doesn't add up to pot. Unless he is getting ripped off?? I think there may have been something more. Why else would he be up during the night? He acts like he is so tired and goes to bed early only to get up after we go to bed - actually I should say after you fall asleep. How can I possibly sleep when I know he is awake and I can hear him at night going through things or going outside? You act irritated if I wake you to tell you one of your kids was outside. Then he would give you b.s. reasons and you actually believed them! If he was high from smoking weed wouldn't he be lazy and hungry? The kid barely eats especially for a preteen boy! And he never slowed down always skating. I never knew anyone in school who stole thousands of dollars and stole things to pawn to buy pot. It doesn't all add up for me.

I am glad he went to boot camp because he had to be sober for that month he was gone. I saw and heard from the other parents though that their kids had to be there longer. Maybe Derek did too. But I don't know what the counselors and therapists said about him. Because no one communicates with the step mom which is all I am and nothing more than a babysitter. I can't even express the disappointment I have and the betrayal I feel.

October 8th

I don't know how to communicate with Mike. I think we are talking about something and agreeing on it but really he just doesn't protest or when I ask him flat out how he feels he says it's fine. Then later I find out he wasn't ok with it but felt I would overpower him anyways. Boy what a great relationship we have! He avoids me and the issues, creating and compounding problems more and more!!!

Since I met him he communicated to me that his birthday wasn't a big deal and he has acted like he doesn't want everyone going all out for him. Every year I feel uncomfortable to celebrate it because he acts like it's just another day and he doesn't want to be in the spotlight. So fine, this year we gave him his gifts the night before (because Roxy wouldn't be there) and then did nothing for him. And now he is mad at me for making him go to a wedding because it was my idea. And all of a sudden we always do what I want. I cannot think of a time when we did something that was my idea. Usually life revolves around the kids and their ideas or he will lay down the law and we will go fish or hunt (his idea). And all of us going to the wedding wasn't totally what I wanted. I wanted a date night with my husband, leave HIS kids home (I didn't have Roxy). It wouldn't have even been a full 24 hours gone. I compromised by agreeing to take his kids. If he didn't want to go I would have went with my friends and left him home to hang out with his kids. OR if he had expressed something he wanted to do on his birthday, I would have done it instead because it was his day. The wedding was for the girl, our mutual friend, who introduced us and made our families come together. I really felt it was important for us to be there no matter what. I did express that to him but now it seems I was a bitch about going. Nothing new, I am starting to get used to this new description of myself.

Mike won't let me know what he wants. I refuse to go back to the way things were yet I am also trying to compromise because I don't want to lose the relationship. I don't want to lose the family either but already feel like I have. Derek is acting superficial about wanting to see me. I think he puts on a charade to make his dad feel ok about the situation between us. He acts like he hugs me but won't really hug me, I have to hug him and his arms just act like they are hugging me but he is like half-assing it and he is all limp. Also he doesn't say he loves me and when he does (in front of his parents usually), he hesitates like he is doing it out of obligation not that he really wants me to know it. I do truly love him and the pain he has caused me is because I love him.

He avoids me if no one else is around and refuses to talk to me. When he has talked to me alone it is angry and defiant. He doesn't listen or acknowledge what I have to say and usually says something about what his parents said…which is the opposite of what I was talking to him about. Both the kids have no respect for me and for quite a while have seen that their parents don't either. I know that we need to work on this I just don't know how. I get very frustrated when I feel that no one is listening to me. When I don't feel validated I keep talking to try to get my point across and in the end feel like an ass. I don't understand why if my husband truly understands me and what I am communicating, he doesn't say it. Or if he doesn't understand why he doesn't say it or even try to figure it out. Or if he thinks I am out of line why he doesn't ask me to step away so we can discuss it without the kids. I just get looks like they all think I am crazy. He has even said he thinks I am bipolar or he said that he wonders about my sanity at times. If he truly understood how I felt and have been feeling for over a year then he might help me not act so crazy.

I think he is crazy but I don't tell him! He might understand why I feel so frustrated if he would take some time to truly listen. He might understand my anger and feelings of being stuck in limbo while he is gone and when he returns with kids that it's hard not to have that catch up time; or that when his son enters the house again my blood boils; or that his refusal to have "us" time is killing me and our marriage. This situation with Derek has been swept under the rug and I believe Mike just wants me to do the same and get over it. Unfortunately what Derek did was in my face for over a year and I knew it in my gut and I had no support and no help and maybe I need this to be addressed and a consequence to be given to move on.

I do not want the kids to leave or not want to be with their dad. I do not think it is good for Mike to not have a relationship with his kids. I do not want them to not feel welcome in my home. I want the kids to feel safe and want to come over when they are grown. I just am having issues that I want to be temporary but will not be temporary if not addressed. If I don't feel safe and no one will address reality then I will have to move out. I cannot continue to feel like me or my daughter are living in an unsafe environment. I will not continue to do damage to my husband and his kids' relationship. If this is not addressed by Christmas I will look for a new place.

October 9th

One thing that has damaged my relationship with Mike the most is that he doesn't take the time to treat me like his wife. I took care of his kids, his house, his bills, everything, and have not felt like he really appreciated me. Now that I don't take care of his kids I feel like he hates me and doesn't want to be married to me. Just because I made my needs clear and my boundaries are set it's like he isn't as in love with me anymore. I also feel like he forgot about our honeymoon. I feel like he will probably never take me on one or if he does it will be way after the kids are gone. Why don't I deserve it? Why don't I deserve being taken out even just once a month? When he takes me fishing on a "date" it's never like a date. Not that he does that very often (maybe 2 times a year). And he concentrates on his fishing, usually doesn't talk much and doesn't even act like he wants to be affectionate.

I no longer like going fishing with him alone because it has no special meaning. There is no romance to it, no communication, it's just doing what he loves to do and I happen to be there too. The last excursion was even to a place that I am totally frightened of getting to. I was shaking with fear the whole way to the freaking place and yes it is cool. I do kinda like how he pushes me to my limits but we didn't really even fish together. Several times I was alone as he was off around another bend. When we have rarely had a few nights without kids he acts like it is up to me to figure out what to do. One time I suggested a movie so we stopped at Redbox but the good ones were gone so we left. I was thinking we would go to another one but we didn't. He drove me home and started in on chores and stuff around the house.

I don't understand why he can't take charge and do something spontaneous like he used to when we were dating. I have gotten so frustrated I have written down ideas for us to do and put them in a jar to choose on the rare occasion we might be alone. However, he hasn't even looked at them as far as I know. It's like he didn't care when I told him about it or just truly doesn't want to take me out anymore. I feel like I do a lot of little romantic things for him but when he has a chance to do something for me he refuses and then acts like it's my fault. I am really starting to feel like there is something wrong with me and I don't understand what is so wrong that I don't deserve love. If and when I leave I am done with men and will NEVER marry again. And I truly mean it this time!!!!!!

October 10th

Affirm: My environment does not determine my state of mind.

Your environment does affect who you are but it does not control you.

October 12th

I am a very detailed person and have been trained to see the small details. In my first job I had to undergo training and if I did not pass I did not work. We had to memorize the menu, memorize how many ounces go into which cups, learn to measure it as accurately as possible and how many scoops of what went into the recipes! It was intense but once I remembered it the job came easily. The bosses know this; a properly trained employee will work efficiently. Also I can remember surprise "white glove inspections". The bosses would come in unexpectedly sometimes during the workday and sometimes at night after we left. They would test surfaces with the white glove and see how well you were cleaning. They had a very detailed list of things they would test and they wouldn't test them all every time, sometimes they would change up the list. You never knew where they would take the white glove so you were always on your toes making sure you were striving for perfection.

And we loved it; the store with the highest score would get a bonus. Monthly bonuses were exciting but even if the boss or owner came in with their family for treats like regular customers, they would give praise and recognition pointing out what you were doing well. Of course it was the same if something was wrong but it was handled discreetly and professionally. It was such a great place to work. I have worked in other places since that didn't really care what you did and the people were miserable to work with. No expectations meant unhappy people. If there was nothing to strive for why would you do anything great or push yourself to do anything extra.

It's crazy how I can tune into the energy of the home and know that someone has been there or something is not right. It's then that my awareness is on high alert; I remember driving into the garage and feeling like the light was bright and just dismissed it as the automatic light that comes on when you open the door. But then when I walk into the house and still sense something odd and that moment when I truly realized something wasn't quite right and go back into the garage to re-examine my initial thoughts, I realize that the actual garage light is left on. I examine everything, the back door is locked and most everything else in the garage appears untouched.

As I come back into the house I notice Derek's door is cracked open a little and I remember that when I put mail in his room yesterday I shut the door completely since it was cold and I didn't want the cold air coming out into the hallway. So I push the door open and realize that my fears are real. There is a binder on the floor, his cabinet is open and his stuff has been moved around since last night. My blood boils; I shut the door and try to think calmly how I will approach this issue.

All of my past attempts at communicating how I feel in regards to him being in my house alone have failed. In fact I have made Mike feel as though I am trying to separate him from his kids. I do not feel that was my intention. In fact I feel that by Derek taking responsibility for himself, he will do better. The fact that his parents are enabling him to just run over to each other's houses at any given time to get what he forgets is so plain for me to see. But I can also understand that as a parent sometimes it is just easier to help your kids out, not lay down firm limits so that you don't have to fight. It's more peaceful when both parents feel the same way.

Then I come along and create chaos because I don't want him in and out of my house at any given time. Well I did allow it for over 3 years actually. But then I realized that my stuff wasn't safe, no one's was actually! When there are no limits, kids feel they can do whatever they want. Without boundaries they don't learn where the safety net is and they can't trust their parents to help them. No wonder he was a mess about feeling unloved. I truly believe that the only reason he didn't admit to stealing from his mom and/or telling her how he really felt was because he felt she would not be there for him and he didn't feel he could lose his mom. She has never set any boundaries and he has said time and time again how insecure he is about her. In the past he has said things that make it clear he doesn't understand why he feels that way though.

When Derek was allowed to roam freely without boundaries, he took whatever he wanted - no matter whose it was. He had no limits and went through every nook and cranny of my personal space. And even after he got caught there was no real consequence to make him look back and think I won't do that again. So the natural consequences that I can enforce at my house are that he will not be allowed in here freely. My trust is broken and he will have to earn it back. And he will not be allowed in here alone. He will have to go out of his way to make sure that I am home before coming over and he will have to ask my permission. I don't necessarily want to shut the door on our relationship but I can no longer take care of a child who is not willing to respect me and my home. I feel until this boundary is firm I cannot welcome him in when I am here.

Recently his actions show that he believes this boundary is not firm and he has come over and let himself in even when I am gone. This disrespect towards me makes it hard to regain the trust. I need space from him to know that he will respect this is my limit. Once I feel he respects my boundaries I will try to invite him in for family time when his Dad is gone. Only at that point do I feel I can start to try and trust him again. And maybe the inconvenience will deter him from making the mistake here again or maybe he will realize how precious trust is to lose. I see it as a good positive thing for him to learn from. Or maybe he will take accountability for his actions or take responsibility for remembering what he will or might need. He has needed this lesson for quite a while.

When I was taking care of him I would try to teach natural consequences but it was never backed up. So anything I said or taught was null and void. In fact I feel that I lost their respect. I still have not been able to get it back, but I believe by Mike enforcing my boundaries and backing me up in front of the kids that they will come back around and give me the respect again.

Evening, Thursday Oct. 13th 2011

Mike said as long as I communicate calmly the reasoning behind taking the key away, that he is ok with it. But then when he backed me up it made me feel angry for other reasons. If he was going to back me up on this he should have done it a while ago when he was home. I feel he should take the key away himself since he is the parent. He needs to enforce the rule so that Derek knows this is the way it is. Usually when I do something it is perceived as flexible because they know their dad (and definitely their mom) will sometimes not enforce what I say or not back me up. So here we go around again.

***

Mike got the call Saturday October 15th about 4:30. He got the job he wanted! After 10 months of resumes, testing, interviewing, and being turned down, now they want him?! They want to know what schedule he wants to work and when he can start. Flurries of questions arise with excitement and hope for a better life! Yes it is out of state but he will be able to commute and possibly be home more than he is now!

He also talked to Tina while I was visiting him up north. They discussed Derek coming in with his key when we are not home. He also talked to Derek and told him to come give me the key to our house. I think this is a very positive change for Mike and hope he truly is going to back me up from here on out. I also hope that he finally realizes he needs to do something to change in order for his son's behavior to change.

Author's Note:

These journal entries were not too long ago and the pain is still present. Derek never did give the key over willingly and continued to come in without permission. Mike refused to take it from him when he came home from working out of town and he started protesting it. I changed the locks despite his insistence not to; he thought his kids shouldn't feel like they are unwelcome in their own house. I gave his daughter a key; it was just his son that I didn't feel should have the right to come in and out freely. We had some lengthy conversations and had a family meeting to outline the rules and consequences.

Mike started taking me out on dates and we even went on a honeymoon for our 4th anniversary. Just last month, things escalated with Mike's daughter, so now I no longer take care of his kids. They are only here when Mike is, which is every two weeks, but it is still very difficult.

I came across a quote today, "all marriages go through good and bad times. If people stick out the rough times, they often find that the relationship improves again." That is my hope, and I am thankful that my husband is committed to our marriage. Otherwise, we wouldn't have survived this storm.

Excerpt Sixteen

March 2012

Post-move.

Post-short-sale.

It was hard. It was difficult. It was sad for me. I felt really depressed about it for a while.

I forgot about depression. Which is good. No complaints on that one. My life is really quite good.

Anyway, boxing stuff up was emotionally hard. I apparently was so stressed that I was sick with a cold basically, just about all month. Plus in January, as well. In the beginning of the month I didn't think I was stressed. Then I got sick. Then I stayed sick. Then I didn't get better. And didn't get better.

Weekend 1: we rented a storage space and thought about moving.

Weekend 2: we moved as much as we could from home-storage, garage, outside shed, etc.

Weekend 3: we moved our bedroom to the new place - with a friend - and started staying there. Also packed up more stuff from the house and put in storage as many boxed items/boxes, etc., as possible.

All week between week 3-4 we went to the house to take care of cats, stray cat, chickens, and to pack more items, pack up the kitchen, the bathroom stuff, etc. it was getting more stressful as we got closer because also it was like, as the house and property got more empty, the pets got more stressed. It was…. sad.

I was sad for them. For me. I was sad about the whole thing on a lot of different levels. ☹

EMOTIONS.

We purchased that home with the intention of staying. For a long time. I felt upset, frustrated, angry, and disappointed about having to/being "forced" into the limited choice of short sale.

ANGER.

Directed outward. At husband. At the situation. At our realtor. At the economic reality. At US for moving to Boise, where apparently I couldn't hold down a job, either.

SAD.

We painted. We remodeled. A little. We landscaped. We planted. A garden, a memorial tree, fruit trees, xeriscaping, strawberries, lavender, and the garden for food, of course, too. Five years of making the soil better and better.

DISAPPOINTED.

We put our hearts into the place. Even though only for about five years, it was our home, with OUR memories. We got kicked out early. ☹

MEMORIES.

Parties. We had some great parties. Indoor winter parties. Outdoor spring and summer and fall parties. Slip-n-slide parties. Birthday parties. Ski patrol parties. Hot tub parties. We put our mattress on the back deck and slept out in summer. We put our mattress by the fireplace and enjoyed a stay-at-home date night. We read by the fire. We cozied up for morning coffee. We cooked together. We had holidays there. We shoveled snow. We took care of it together. Did yard work together. Projects together. We came home to THAT house together.

Like a lost loved one, that's all gone now. But, lost, gone, like it can never be again. It was heartbreaking.

For a few weeks my heart was broken.

I was so depressed I went to work, came home at 3 every day and went to bed. I didn't cook dinner for anyone or do anything around the house. I suspect it was annoying. But I couldn't help it in the moment. I was soooo sad.

I wanted to write about it when it was more depressing and in the moment… but didn't feel like doing anything. The world was dead to me and monochrome for a while.

I felt bad for myself, for us… and I also felt bad for the millions of other Americans going through the same thing but possibly with worse situations… maybe with kids, or with health problems. Maybe people without friends to let them stay with them.

I remember reading an article last year in the Readers' Digest which profiled 3 or 4 families that had to short sell or foreclose and move in with others or into a motel… with their kids! I mean seriously, it could always be worse. I couldn't imagine having to move into a motel with 3 kids and having to leave the family dog at the pound because of this type of thing. Totally heartbreaking.

Our situation was sad, too… but not abominable. Somewhere in the middle of the scale… it can almost always be worse, and it could always be better…

Excerpt Seventeen

I hate my father. Isn't that a strange thing to say? Not what you expected is it? Well, he's not your typical everyday run of the mill father. And I'm certainly not your typical everyday run of the mill kid.

Don't get preachy with me about loving my parents. You haven't heard the whole story, so maybe you shouldn't judge. Not that I blame you, with me dropping it on you like that, but I wanted to get your attention.

First, let me tell you about me. I'm twelve. People tell me I'm smart, which is true. They also say I'm standoffish, which is probably true, but I've got my reasons. I'm kind of an outcast. The kids at school don't anymore know what to do with me, than I do them. Most of them come from normal, dysfunctional families, so it ends up sorta being like we live on different planets. They make fun of me; I act like it doesn't matter. Of course it does matter, but I'm not going to let them know that.

At home I just kinda disappear into the woodwork most of the time. I've got three brothers who don't live here anymore, and a seventeen year old sister, who does. If I ever end up in front of a firing squad, she'll spend her last dime buying a ticket to watch. We don't get along real well. My mom and I don't exactly hit it off either. The only one I can count on is, or rather was, the dog.

Cathy, (that's my sister) brought the dog home with her a couple of months ago. Some weirdly mixed cute little mongrel puppy. In a rare moment of consensus, we decided to name her Ding-a-Ling. I know, dumb name for a dog, but she did not win intelligence contests. She was nice to have around. She'd lie in wait, and attack the bottom of my bell bottom jeans. The way she got into it, you'd have thought she was a fearless bear dog closing in on a wounded grizzly. It was nice to have somebody to play with. It was nice to have somebody to hold. She cuddled really well for a dog with only three operational brain cells. When I was feeling generally awful, it felt good to hold her just because she was warm and soft and alive. It didn't really matter that she wasn't very smart. It mattered that she was there. At least she was there, for a little while.

When Cathy first brought her home, I didn't think Dad would let me keep her. I expected him to pitch a tizzy and order us to get rid of her right off the bat. He's like that, usually, a grade A bastard. Good old Dad. I'm the only one of his kids that call him that. The rest of them call him "Ernie." The way they say it makes it sound like a swear word. I call him "Dad" because it makes him happy. I figure it's a good idea to make him happy, seeing's as how he's bigger than I am.

Actually, he's bigger than most people. Of course, my perception is a bit slanted. He's really only about 5' 10". It's just that he's scarier than most people. When he gets mad and starts yelling, his eyes get really big, and fiery black. You get the feeling that he's sorta lost it, and there's just a possibility that this time he's gonna kill somebody.

Anyway, he didn't say much when Cathy brought the dog home. No yelling, no swearing, no threats, no nothing. It was kind of unnerving. The first few days I felt like I was living on a minefield. Walk softly, talk as little as possible, and hope the old man doesn't go thermonuclear on you. But he didn't. He didn't act like he really liked the puppy, but he didn't act like he hated her, either. Gradually, I started to relax and believe everything was okay. That was my first mistake. Over the next few weeks, I made my second mistake.

My second mistake was getting attached. She was only a damn dog, after all. But let's face it. When you can count all the friends you have in the world on one thumbnail, a dog looks pretty good. So, I admit it. I loved her. Burn me at the stake. Do anything you have to do, but teach that girl not to be stupid. With my best interests at heart, dear old Dad set out to do just that.

It isn't often that Mom and Cathy and I go anywhere together, but we did that day. I know we went shopping, but I can't remember for what. That was the third mistake. Strike three - you're out. Never leave Dad home alone with anything you care about. Not if it is something he can kill.

Ding-a-Ling didn't run up to meet us like she usually did. She was usually right there, all ears and feet and tongue, making sure I knew she was glad I was home. She didn't come when I called her, either. That's when I started to worry. It didn't take long to find the blood, spattered around the ground in the back yard next to the fence.

Knowing my father as well as I do, the first thing I did was run into the house and demand to know what he had done to my puppy. In a truly touching scene, right out of Father Knows Best, he vehemently defended his innocence, largely for the benefit of a couple of his friends, who happened to be visiting. He suggested perhaps a large hawk had gotten the puppy, since she was so small.

I know, I told you I was smart, but for a smart kid, I can be awfully damned gullible. I believed him. Imagining her lying wounded somewhere, I went off to look for my puppy. As it turned out, Cathy had already found her. I had just gotten back out in the yard, when Cathy came walking out of the field carrying Ding-a-Ling, or rather, the bloody pulpy mess that used to be Ding-a-Ling. Dad hadn't shot her. That is what he had usually done in the past. One well aimed shot from the 30-06 and hey presto... watch the kid cry over one more dog. Dingy must have been too small for him to waste the ammunition. He'd taken a hammer and bashed her brains in.

That was the first and only time I ever hit my father. I very calmly walked back into the house and punched him in the nose as hard as I could. It was a good thing he had company, or he'd have killed me. As it was, he just didn't talk to me for a week.

My mother helped us bury the puppy. I don't remember where. I remember mom leaning on the shovel and crying. That's strange, because she never had before. She asked if we wanted to go down to the river. Cathy said no, but I went.

Mom and I went to the river. We didn't talk. We didn't even stay together. I went off alone and sat on a rock next to the water. I didn't cry; just sat and stared at nothing. It's not that I didn't hurt. O God, I hurt. It's that it didn't matter, one way or the other. I sat there for a long time. For some reason, I threw a piece of wood in the water. The current caught it and I watched it drift away until it was gone. Then I walked back to the car and we went home.

I hate my father. It isn't so surprising anymore, is it? But I know it still bothers you that I am so matter of fact about the whole thing. What do you want me to do? Cry? Get mad? Beat the ground and pour ashes over my head? It wouldn't change anything. I hate him, but I still have to live here. Someday he'll be dead, you know. He'll be dead and there will be time enough to cry.

Excerpt Eighteen

Author's Introduction:

These were all written directly after my friend, Timothy, committed suicide.

February 2009

Talking with you was like talking to myself. What will become of me?

I want to call you every time I am really angry or really excited. When I need to vent I'm like, god, I've got to call Tim. He will listen and he'll get it but most importantly he will understand and because he understands and never judges I will feel valued. Because I feel valued I will, naturally, feel better after talking to him. I want to call him and tell him about Craig last night. Who else can I tell all my weird sexual stories to? Who else will listen and understand? And then I remember. Oh.....I can't call you. You are not there.

My biggest fear is this, Timothy: I am so afraid that I am going to forget how you made me feel. So afraid I am going to forget what pure love feels like. So afraid my heart is going to close back up – that what you gave me will go away. I need you to sustain it. You can never completely leave me. You must always stay around me or in me. It doesn't mean you can't cross over, or whatever, it just means that your essence, what you gave me, what you put into me, that love, can never ever go away.

I also know that what I felt with you – what we had together – the way we felt toward each other – was meant to only be felt between you and me. I know that what I had with you is too sacred for words – too deep. Most people will never know this kind of love. It was, is, ours and ours alone meant for no other two. Unique, bittersweet. You were everything to me.

March 2009

Different renditions of the same.

There was a mirror on the ceiling right above the bed. When you were sleeping next to me, I would look up into the mirror just so that I could see you sleeping there next to me. I could inspect every piece of you and you wouldn't know I was watching you.

When we slept together in Naomi's bed I used to watch you sleep. When I was afraid that my gaze would wake you up I turned and looked up at the mirror that hung over the bed. That way I could watch you and you wouldn't know.

One night the rats in that attic were crawling around, scurrying, looking for food. They woke us up. Do you remember that?

I still remember how you looked in that mirror. So angelic, so serene, so beautiful. Is this also how you looked in death? Is this how you looked when Naomi found you hanging from the rafters?

You were the most beautiful thing I had ever laid eyes on. Watching you sleep in the mirror I thought I had died and gone to heaven. That I was there among the angels. I could almost hear them singing every time I looked at you and see their angelic light shining through your eyes.

***

I was so distraught I did not date anyone.

I can still see your eyes
I feel you look into me
Go into me

With those eyes
You move through me like the wind
But softer
Swirling around like an intoxicating fog
I am overcome
With you

And when you touch me
We go into each other
All boundaries of time and space disappear
I can feel you know as I write this
Somewhere beyond yet still with me
It's like our bodies aren't even bodies anymore
Physical dimensions fall away
When you touch me and go into me

It's not that I *would* never hurt you it is that I **could** never hurt you. To hurt you and to see you hurt is more than I can bear. When I told you that I could never hurt you I meant it. To deny you only causes me great pain and suffering. To try to sever our bond, complete despair.

I don't want to cry yet. I look so pretty. Make up and all. Feel like you are feeding me. My skin feels tingley and alive. It is like you are all over me. So strong it almost makes me feel sick.

I don't want to talk to anybody……

***

I remember that morning as if it were yesterday. Well I remember the phone call anyways. The rest is a fucking blur. Amanda texted me and asked if I were alright. I was irritated. Why the fuck wouldn't I be alright? I thought there was some stupid drama going on between Naomi and Timothy and somehow people were talking about me or whatever. Too damn old for this high school shit. I called her and said, "Why wouldn't I be alright?" Like I said, I was irritated.

She said, "Jacki, I have to tell you something." I could feel it in her voice.

"What. Tell me." She began to cry.

What is it? Tell me.

Timothy killed himself last night.

What? Disbelief.

Then I screamed. I screamed "No!!!!!" No no no no no no no no no no no no and collapsed to the ground.

My two daughters were in the next room.

***

I was not the one who found you, yet the image of you hanging there haunts me and lingers in my mind. Even though I didn't see it I can see it. The image of the black tie that you wore that night wrapped around your neck. They said it was something black around your neck. I am not sure it was the same tie I saw you wearing hours earlier. That tie seemed a bit short and weak to hold the weight of your beautiful body without breaking itself. I think it would have broken before your neck broke but they said your neck broke instantly – oh the horror of the image – the horror of you – YOU, delicate, precious you. . . hanging lifeless, limp, body swaying back and forth. Lifeless. From the attic rafters. I wonder what the expression on your face was. I wish I would have been the one to find you. I heard that you were white and blue. You had been there awhile before Naomi came home and found you. She looked at you, stunned, not registering what she was looking at for a moment. The way it did not register when Amanda told me that you committed suicide last night. Naomi looked at you and began to scream. I listened to Amanda's words, "Tim killed himself last night" and began to scream. She turned and ran out of the room, out of the house, down the street screaming. I turned from standing in the kitchen facing my children and ran into the other room, sat down on the couch and screamed.

Author's note:

Timothy was my friend. He was the most beautiful thing that I had ever laid eyes on. He had this incredible wavy blonde hair that he would toss about carelessly; a long, thin, sinewy body; an infectious laugh; and the most piercing, intense hazel eyes. I remember those eyes. Those big, hazel eyes. He pierced right through me with those searching eyes. Right down into my core. Timothy could see me; see into me. He knew me. For the first time in my life, I had met someone who really could see me.

Timothy was bisexual, more gay than bisexual if you ask me, but he did not like to be identified solely based on his sexual preference. He was 16 years younger than me and I was in love with him. He was the most compassionate, gentle creature that I have ever met. I often wondered if he were human. He seemed much more like an angel than a human being. My heart was cold, sewn shut, before I met him. Timothy is the man, boy, really, who showed me how to love. It is because of him. Because he was not afraid to pour love into people, to be vulnerable, to love deeply and purely, that I opened my heart to allow love to come into my life. This type of love was gentle, soft, passionate, divine. I had not known this even existed until I met him. And then he was yanked from me and it was gone.

When he died he did not leave a note. I saw him that night. Just hours before it happened. We had been fighting. We spoke and made amends. We were supposed to meet for coffee the next day to finish our discussion. I never saw him again.

His mother was a drug addict who used with him; his father disowned him; his sister died in a car accident; his brother drowned; his boyfriend consistently cheated on him. People fucked him over left and right. Such a pure soul. It is disgusting to me how people treat the pure of heart.

I do not know why he hung himself that evening. His life was shit, I will give him that, but I do not think that is why he chose to die. I think it was much deeper than that. I think he was too pure, too light, too ethereal for this world. There is a quote by Friedrich Nietzsche that says, "The world is too much for me, then and now." I believe this is why Timothy took his life. The world tried to devour him. I think his light was too much for the world. To watch all of the horror of life, all of the cruelty, all of the ugliness, all of the deception, well, it was just too unbearable for him.

The night he died. I felt it. A wave of peace passed over me. My cat meowed and looked up into the space directly above his kitty head. My room became very still. I was sitting on the bed with my two children. I said, "Timothy? Is that you?" The next morning, I got the phone call.

Excerpt Nineteen

06.12.1995

When the cold metal of the blade touches my skin, I shiver. It's my best-friend. We have no secrets. When we are together, we are one. When I press the blade against my flesh there is no resistance. The stinging pain fills me with a warmth I can't describe. My skin opens like the parting of the sea. Blood springs to the surface marking its path. I can breathe. The pain of being me is freed. I push the blade deeper and drag it further across my skin. I hiss with the pleasure it brings. I lift the blade and begin again.

I tried to cover up the cuts from last night as I always did. A few people at school saw them. I didn't care. I lost track of how many times I'd cut myself over the last few months. One girl asked me why I did that to myself. I told her it feels good and that it's hard to explain. She looked at me like a freak. I rolled my eyes, she wouldn't understand. Hell, I didn't even understand, not really or completely!

People think it's for attention. I'm sure for some it is, but not me. I don't walk around with my scars hanging out, parading them like a prize. I feel ashamed. Ashamed I'm so... it's my escape from life.

I feel so... so sad all the time. Lost. I hate who I am. I feel trapped inside like the real me is in there waiting to get out, if I only cut deeper.

Marci my sister calls me fat because she's skinny. I know I'm not fat, though it hurts to hear her say that. I know the truth though, she would be bigger than me if she didn't starve herself. Grandma Smith calls me stupid because reading and spelling are difficult for me. I tried one time to explain it to her, that when I read the words do a dance in my head and some of the words don't all show up to join. She didn't care. My mom and dad work all the time. I never really see them. But it's okay. I have Grandpa Smith. He's my angel.

Today when he picked me up from school he could see I was not myself and he frowned at me. It was an odd thing to see. Grandpa Smith was one of the happiest people in my life. He taught me to use my hands and to use my head. Marci hates that we're close. She doesn't say it, yet I see it in her eyes.

Grandpa asked me what was wrong. I told him I didn't know, only that I was sad inside. I could never hide things from him. I didn't want too. His mouth pressed to a thin line and his eyes squinted at the corners. "I'll take care of that," he declared.

Next thing I know we're pulling into the Thrifty's parking lot.

He says, "Ice cream can fix anything." I couldn't help but smile. In his eyes I'm sure he thought it could. He had a sweet tooth bigger then my head.

We walked inside and stood at the ice cream counter. He put his arm around my shoulder and whispered into my ear. "If I see you cutting yourself again there'll be no more ice cream for you again. Not with me."

I swallowed hard and hot tears burned the backs of my eyes. We waited for some time before someone saw us standing at the counter. Grandpa Smith never complained, just kept his arm around me. I croaked out my order to the clerk as did grandpa when he appeared. Then we walked out to the car. When we got in I couldn't hold back the tears. I didn't want grandpa to be upset with me. Ever.

Grandpa, I said, "I'm sorry. I don't know why I do it. I don't want to, but I can't stop."

We sat in the small pickup truck. I cried and licked my ice cream. Grandpa didn't say anything only licked his cone too. I thought I was going to die right there in the truck. Shame filled me. What was wrong with me?

"You are my rose." Grandpa said in between licks, "You have thorns and sometimes can prick others deeply. No matter how others try and cut you down, you grow back, thicker and stronger than before. So just remember when you're sad... You're my rose."

I couldn't swallow. A lump the size of an orange had formed in my throat. I was his rose! After he said that, my world brightened.

Author Note:

I was fourteen with an athletic build and had dyslexia at this time in my life. And as you have read I was very lost. Looking back now, I know I was trying to find my place in the world and to know I was loved by someone. My Grandpa Smith was my rock and the one person I never wanted to disappoint. He died when I was 29. A little light went out in me the day he died, but I carry him with me always. All it takes is one angel to save you from yourself. Who is your angel?

Excerpt Twenty

Author's note:

These journals were from 2010 when I was going through a separation from my husband just weeks after our first and only child was born. I cut out a lot of things that I felt weren't a part of a good read in order to get to the point of something others could relate to. These journals are a representation of the journey I went through of accepting my reality of my husband leaving, his mental condition, then me finally having the courage to leave him for good as I began to discover myself again without his dysfunction in my life. Recognizing the qualities that made me who I was, and someone I identified with, was part of this process, as I had lost a lot of those qualities throughout my unhealthy attachment to someone who was, in the end, manipulative and emotionally abusive. I hope to bring understanding and validation to others who have gone, or are going though, a similar experience of recognition and discovery.

July 16th

The facts:

My husband left me and my newborn child earlier this week. After an argument over his behavior and choices that I can't seem to even put on electronic paper, he took the car, which I told him he could have since I won't need it or want to pay for it with him gone. I just found out today that he also took my credit card, which was my only way to pay for my needs. A few days ago I was at Whole Foods buying more prenatal vitamins and some probiotics for Violet, when I noticed the card was missing from my wallet at the register. Luckily, I had just enough room on another credit card to pay the total and was thanking my lucky stars that I wasn't at the register at the grocery store where my total would have been far more than $35 and I would have been mortified to say, "Sorry, I can't pay for these because my dead-beat-baby-daddy stole my credit card." When I got home I checked the charges on the card online and, sure enough, they were down where Gabriel fled to; the south of the state.

Gabriel's mom keeps trying to come over to see Violet and talk to me. I let her come over on Tuesday, but it was really hard. She wants to come over on Sunday, and the only reason I may let her is because she is going to pick up more of Gabriel's belongings, which I don't want here. With the help of my friends, my mom and my step-dad, I have been able to get most of Gabriel's clothes and books packed up. I am grateful to have the extra room and peace that is coming from not having his things here reminding me of what isn't, and from not having him break my heart and family 1-2 times a week by me not being able to accept that he isn't a part of our lives anymore. I think that by next Monday, it will be the first time he hasn't done so since December, and it will only be because he is not here to manipulate me. I am looking forward to celebrating that week of freedom on Monday.

Last Night's Dream:

Last night I dreamt of abuse and betrayal. Someone I trust and love took advantage of my weak will, knowing who and what had left me broken. My body, numb and uncaring, allowed them. At first I just felt unable to fight back. Eventually, however, my sad heart, tired of being thrown away, craved the love; dysfunctional and temporary though I knew it was. I was well aware of the pain that would follow, remembering from the past how it would leave an even deeper hole than what had been before, but I didn't care. I was too addicted to the feeling of being loved and even though everything inside of me was screaming to not trust who I thought I could, he was proving that my resolve to take the abuse was his greatest weapon. I realized that no matter how many bruises he had left on my life, it was as if I believed that no wrong he ever did, would ever be wrong enough for me.

I awoke and immediately knew who and what the dream was about. Gabriel had texted me from a number unknown to me the day before, just telling me that he was thinking about me and wondered if we could talk. I hated that I got little butterflies in my stomach at just the thought that he was thinking of me. They were definitely fainter and had a bitter aftertaste, but they were still there. I am grateful that this dream gave me quite the visual of what I have allowed him to do and be for the past 5 ½ years in my life, and that I can't keep hanging on to the boy who I only knew for 6 months before I committed to be his forever. I have been fighting to get that person back for 5 years. It's time that I realize, if I can be delusional enough to allow myself to keep inviting this pain back into my life, then I could certainly fool myself into loving someone that I made up in my mind during those 6 months, or someone that he is choosing not to be. Even though he never physically hit me, the emotional abuse, manipulation and continual stream of lies is enough for anyone to feel like nothing. Sometimes I almost wished he would have hit me so that his abuse would have been more obvious and a definite line would have been crossed. Also, I wouldn't be able to hide the dysfunction in our relationship from anyone anymore. Instead of me choosing who to talk to about things because I didn't want them to unfairly judge the situation, someone around me would have stepped in and did what I couldn't do for myself.

Now I have a newborn daughter who is just as affected by my insane relationship choices…and look what I have done. I have made a mess of her life as well as mine before she even arrived in this world. But I know that it is because of her that I am finally able to let go and even push Gabriel out of our lives if I have to. For some reason, I was able to justify him hurting me over and over again. But when it comes to affecting Violet's life and well-being, even if it is because Gabriel brings such stress into my life, which makes me a worse mom, I have finally had the reason to say, "Stop," and mean it. I am scared to death of raising this child by myself. But I know that it will be easier to do without him in our lives and I owe it to Violet to make the best of what we have. I will always be indebted to her, because she saved my life.

July 19th

Today Violet and I went to the campus bookstore to pick up my textbooks for fall semester. It felt great to get out of the apartment and do something independently. After we got home I heard the doorbell from Violet's room where I was taking her out of her car seat, followed by what sounded like the doorknob jiggling. I thought Gabriel was here and I can't deny the feelings I felt. I was nervous, scared, upset and protective of Violet all at the same time. I opened the door I found a package was sitting there between the screen and front door. The ruckus was just from the UPS man. It made me realize that I am so grateful that Gabriel is in Las Vegas and I am glad that I cancelled the credit card; otherwise he may have come back to Salt Lake City since he would have had the means. I was reminded of the possibility of starting new and having good things accompany that feeling because the credit card came a day early and the $100 check from a survey I took for the university came in the mail today as well. Good thoughts are few and far between these days, but they exist. That is enough to help get me though each day for now.

July 20th

Just as I thought Gabriel couldn't bring me down again by making me feel worthless & ugly, like something you would kick down the street like unimportant trash, it happens. I went into his Hotmail account today to get the link to pay a bill, when I see over 10 emails from AdultFriendFinder.com where he set up a profile and has received emails from women who are "interested" or want him to view their "hot steamy photos." He has, in the last 3 days, created a profile on that website, reactivated his MySpace page and changed his status to "single" and changed his status on Facebook to "it's complicated." This is all after I let him know that if he wanted to talk to me I was willing to communicate on instant messenger. He told me that he couldn't because he "didn't have access to the internet." I was so hurt and upset that I wanted to email him or change his status on the Facebook account to say "It's really not complicated...you left your wife and newborn child for pot and porn." Instead, I forwarded all said emails to my Yahoo account and put them in a folder to use against him in court, should I have to.

Gabriel's mom is still buying his lies and helping him out by letting him stay at her house and having him "work" for money to give to me for paying bills. She said that she was giving me all of the money he earned to pay bills/expenses with. Some of the emails were confirmations for paid porn, so I am not sure where he could have gotten the money from if it wasn't her. I am pretty sure she is giving him money for "gas" or "snacks" or whatever. I wish she would wake up and kick him out so that he can, as step-dad says, "meet Jesus."

Violet is doing so well. We are starting to establish a schedule and routine. She notices faces and things that are within 3 feet now. She loves to lie on her play mat and look at the lights and sounds. She also falls asleep so well in her sling when I take a short walk around the court. She is wonderful.

July 23rd

By the suggestion of my aunt, I have looked into a possible cause for Gabriel's severe mood swings.

Mayoclinic.com: Bipolar Disorder.

Manic phase of bipolar disorder. Signs and symptoms can include:

- Euphoria
- Extreme optimism
- Inflated self-esteem
- Poor judgment
- Rapid speech
- Racing thoughts
- Aggressive behavior
- Agitation or irritation
- Increased physical activity
- Risky behavior
- Spending sprees or unwise financial choices
- Increased drive to perform or achieve goals
- Increased sex drive
- Decreased need for sleep
- Inability to concentrate
- Careless or dangerous use of drugs or alcohol
- Frequent absences from work or school
- Delusions or a break from reality (psychosis)
- Poor performance at work or school

Depressive phase of bipolar disorder: Signs and symptoms can include:

- Sadness
- Hopelessness
- Suicidal thoughts or behavior
- Anxiety
- Guilt
- Sleep problems
- Low appetite or increased appetite
- Fatigue
- Loss of interest in daily activities
- Problems concentrating
- Irritability
- Chronic pain without a known cause
- Frequent absences from work or school
- Poor performance at work or school

…It's like they know my husband as I do.

July 31st

Gabriel and I went to our 1st marriage counseling appointment this year. It was about a year ago that we were going to a marriage counselor and to a relationship course. The only thing that is not explainable by the Bipolar Disorder is how much Gabriel lies to me or keeps the whole truth from me. Yesterday he talked about how he doesn't lie to me anymore at our 4 o'clock marriage counseling appointment. We then came home and he packed up his stuff and left to go back to Enterprise to pick up some more of his things. Within the hour he was at his cousin's house smoking pot for hours and probably drinking, even though he also said that he wouldn't drink and drive anymore (since he did it a week ago).

We suspected that Gabriel had Bipolar Disorder a week ago and it was actually confirmed on Thursday by 2 psychiatrists, who also confirmed that he is in an extreme manic state. He was prescribed some medications and I am hopeful that these will help. It would be great if at least we were able to hold a day-to-day conversation. Right now we can't do that without him also talking about how it is related to the whole world or how his childhood is a paradox or how he wants to grow a garden for a living. It is very hard to not be able to have a conversation with my best friend. I miss him greatly.

August 12th

Dear Gabriel,

I see your suffering, I see your pain. I don't know it as my own, but I know that it is very real behind your eyes. I want to heal you. But I know you are not mine to heal. I want to be everything you need, the only thing you require. But I know I am not your savior, nor your miracle. I want to be with you while you follow your light and leave the dark behind. But I know that I don't need to be by your side forever to feel that I did good by you. I want to be what you want, but I know that role is unclear. I know that I will miss you, but I know that you were never mine to have. So here I stand, knowing there will be times that you need me and I won't be there. But I have to also know that there will also be times when you don't want me around, so it all works out somehow.

I am sorry for your suffering, I am so sorry for that. I wish more than anything that I could take away your pain and your hurt from the past, present and future. I wish more than anything that you could be who you desire to be, without all of the extra things going on in your head.

Maybe we are better off as friends, so that I can help you without either of us feeling guilty for constantly hurting each other. I am not sure if I am strong enough to just be your friend and not your lover, but we will see. As I said once in the past, I just need to get through this part, and then we will see about what's next. Violet will know of you, I will never pretend you never existed. You may be one of the most beautiful things to bless her life.

August 17th

I am confused. I know that I can't put my faith in what Gabriel says when he is in his rational states now, because they don't happen very often and he is not capable of holding up to the things he says. He needs to become stable on his own before I can accept him back into my life and Violet's life again. I know this. But he is my weakness, and I want to believe him every time he promises me what I have always wanted: a happy, functional life with him. I am not trying to be unrealistic about the ups and downs of relationships, but the fact that it would be something new to not feel helpless and abused at least once a week, is something that must not go unnoticed. I haven't felt whole for an entire week in 2010, maybe I haven't felt whole once in our marriage. I pushed many memories out of my mind so that I wouldn't see the writing on the wall. I knew there was something there to be interpreted. I never thought it could be a mental illness in Gabriel, but whatever it was, I knew it would spell out: leave Gabriel, and I never was willing to accept that.

August 26th

My heart aches for the decision that I can feel settling into my mind and heart. Though it is hard for me to accept now, I am beginning to. Gabriel is unstable, and really two different people.

I feel very connected to one person, and another I feel like I nearly hate, because that person treats me like their enemy. It is very hard to feel so loved and hated by the same person. I know the good comes with the bad; I just need to remind myself that the saying was not specifically talking about someone whose moods are so unstable. I need to remember that daily. I miss him. I hope he is safe, though it has been good for me to not be able to contact him right now. He is my addiction that fate has pulled away from me temporarily for my sake and sanity. I love him and will always wish the best for him. I hope he always knows that, past, present and future. I have so much love for him. But I know that even if not today, I must leave him.

August 27th

I know there are some things that I will have to accept that will happen, perhaps before I feel prepared for them to, and before I think that I can feel the full weight of the consequence of my choice. Even so, I am working to accept these things so that my decision can be complete and encompassing.

To Gabriel:

In my decision about ending our relationship, I willingly accept the following consequences:

I know that you will blame me for the meds that you took because you say they are what made you crazy and caused us to be in this situation, but I will know that, by doing so, you are not accepting your part in this in the past or present, even if we don't count anything that happened in our relationship this year.

I know that you will make me new promises that I will want to believe this time, but I will know that they are nothing new, and as much as I want to believe you, you will not be able to keep those promises.

I know that you will also blame me for the things that, in truth, you are guilty of contributing, but I will know that you are just upset.

I know that you will be so hurt and that you will say things like, "I can't do this without you," and "If you are not in my life, I have nothing." This will hurt me a lot to hear and will make me want to change my mind, but I will know that you will be okay. In fact, I think that being on your own will give you less stress and allow you to live a life that is more flexible for your moods.

I know you will not want to move out and you may quit your degree program, but I will know that it is your choice and if you don't want to or can't do it without me, then I don't want you doing it at all because I can't carry the leftover of what you can't handle. I have set myself up so that I am making a life for myself to do what I am passionate about and it will also support me and our daughter.

I know you will be so sad to not be living with and sharing in the joy of Violet, but I will know that allowing you to live your life how you want to then letting her in when you can afford it emotionally will be healthier for her and you. I will also know that not having to pick up your slack will make me a better mother.

I know you will want to try again to make it work, but I will know that the stress of our relationship that made me physically ill before school even started was a sure sign that I don't stand a chance of being around to take care of Violet without major health problems in my life unless I take care of the things that are bringing unneeded stress.

I know I will miss you and that this will be, by far the hardest thing I will ever have to do, but I will know that it is not only the best thing for me, it is the best thing for our family, and surely the best thing for you.

I know you will want to be mad and act like you don't want me around, but I will know that if you are willing, I would always want to maintain a friendship with you. It is what I want and it will be better for Violet if we maintain a healthy relationship, free from contention and contempt.

I know you love me, and you may love me more than anyone else ever will, but I will know that this is what I want and more importantly…what I need.

September 6th

I spoke with you today. At first you seemed so distant, so selfish. Then, after you had broken down and began to cry, and cry…and cry, I felt you have begun to understand. My heart, though it began to feel its old, familiar spark today, is still numb. I can't feel for you right now, I'm not sure that I ever will again.

I have had to build a strong resolve in order to deal these past couple of weeks, and I am not sure it will be broken. It is fairly strong, as resolves go. I should know, I have been working on it ever since the first time you left a wound on my heart that began to scar. And as much as I wanted to ignore the hurt, there was that pretty, puckering scar. Horrible and worse than it may have been, had I not ignored it.

And now you are asking for me to accept you back, even worse, I fear you may be asking me to accept your behavior back.

It seems that in the end we were both set to please each other so much that we lost what we wanted as progressing individuals. The person I am trying to rebuild: the person I was so long ago, I am not sure if you will want to be with; simply because, you don't know this person. Who am I? Well, let's see if I can decipher that for you. I will have to think back to my past to get a full answer to that question.

When crossed, I am a fiery woman, a force to be reckoned with.

I am a speaker of peace and positivity.

I am a poet and a seeker of truth and beauty. I love to discover it and I love to write about it. I fear tapping into this talent again, because I still remember what it was to share it with those who understood, and I miss them dearly. In not writing, I continually mourn their passing from my life.

I am spiritual and lovely, one who enjoys communing with those who see the world in the way that I do: as a possibility. Nothing is out of my reach. I believe that it is in realizing this that I see how I can be my greatest strength or my worst enemy.

I enjoy feeling the Universe as a means to create beauty in my life: tangible beauty and satisfaction and happiness. I neither fear nor stress for my future. I know that putting out beauty will bring it back, and I am determined to get it back.

I love being a mother and a friend. I enjoy teaching others who desire to hear of my knowledge. Perhaps not yet wisdom, but I am adding to that bank every day.

I enjoy being around people who share my affinity for all things spiritual. I enjoy meditating and wish I did it more. I know that great power and possibility are at my fingertips when I practice this seemingly simple task. I know that I have talents and strengths that I have not yet begun to know and understand, but that I will once I master this ritual.

I love to sing and feel the spirit that accompanies music. I want to be the lead singer of a band. It would be so much fun. So far, the Universe has brought a guitar player, a bass player and, most recently, a drummer into my larger circle of acquaintances. The problem is, the guitar player likes to sing, the bass player isn't really into the kind of music that I would like to sing and I don't think anyone takes me seriously. But I will continue to work on it.

Inside, I am just an excited child who is easily fascinated by sparkly things and things of possibility. It gets me into trouble now just as much as it did when I was a child on the outside. Others seem to love my passion for life, but I know that sometimes it is just me being naïve on purpose…because life is more exciting when we leave a little to be discovered for another day.

Excerpt Twenty One

Author's Intro:

Diary From Crazyland: This series of journal entries captures me buried in depression and anxiety, knee deep in psych meds, and struggling to make sense of it all.

04.04.2010

I write, not because someone thinks I should, but because it will leave proof that I am here - that I tried to find meaning even though the world made no sense. I write to say to the darkness "I didn't give up."

04.05.2010

I don't want to put out the effort today, to think about what matters. I'm so tired. And what does it matter, anyway? My life is full of details that are utterly meaningless. Today, I moved files around, and set up some processing parameters. I started testing Janice's setup for a new account. Did any of it matter? Will it matter twenty years from now? Maybe I'm a bit bummed tonight.

04.07.2010

I am freaked out and looking for comfort that isn't there. I can't stop munching, because I am lost, and I don't want to feel my lostness. It is me, screaming when I cannot scream. I am function, I am not as anxious as I was - but nothing stops the terror of being alone.

04.13.2010

I avoid writing most of the time. Why? Because writing is the only truly honest thing that I do. And honest means feeling what is inside. What abandonment is greater than when you abandon yourself?

04.14.2010

So - the company took on a new account that I should have been assigned to. I was not. Janice came in, and announced to LeAnne - "I won the bet!" They went on to discuss it, as if I was not there. It was obvious I was not to be included in the conversation. I am the defective one. I can't do my job. I left work screaming inside. I know I am not my job - I know I am more than that - but what do I do RIGHT? I am failing. I want to hide forever. I don't want to do this anymore.

04.17.2010

What can I do? There's the question. The whole world is alien. I function in it, because I have no choice, but it is not willingly. I don't give up, just because I don't know how.

So, there's the truth.

04.19.2010

I was up for all of five minutes this morning before I started seeing things. The alarm went off at quarter to four, and like always, I shut it off as soon as it started to beep. I swung out of bed, and was surprised to step on my fuzzy blanket, which was on the floor at the foot of the bed. Stepping carefully to avoid tripping over it (it was much too early to think of picking it up), I went into the bathroom and turned on the light. This is my morning routine. Up, walk carefully to avoid tripping over discarded clothing, pillows, or (my personal favorite) Greg's belt, which he sometimes drops right where I walk. Nothing says I love you quite like a belt hook in your foot at four in the morning. Turn on the bathroom light, start the water so that it can warm up... pee... wash face... pull on socks that have been left out on the stand in the bathroom, and then go back in the bedroom to get work out shoes. The bathroom is right next to the bedroom, so there is a reasonable amount of light.

The work out shoes are tucked in the corner on the other side of Annie's big round bed. I get down on my knees, and give her a big hug and some pets and kisses before I reach over her and grab them. This is where it all went wrong, because laying next to Annie on the cushion was one of her paws, severed. I didn't scream, although my heart actually stopped beating. I jumped up, flipped on the light next to the bed, and ran back over to her. She was fine, and I counted all four of her paws right where they were supposed to be. She knew I was upset, so she tucked her head up under my chin and I held her until my heart rate came back down to semi normal. I switched on auto pilot, and reached over and grabbed the shoes.

Annie followed me into the living room and tucked her head under my arm as I was putting them on. She usually stays in bed a little longer, 'til she knows I'll be ready to let her out, but like I said, she knew I was upset. I was going to let her out, but was suddenly afraid of the bad people in the world who would torture a sweet fuzzy goofball like Annie. Our yard is surrounded by a combination of six foot chain link and wood fencing, and I make sure that all four gates are securely padlocked, even the ones that go to the driveway. Nonetheless, I grabbed a jacket, and wearing underwear and tennis shoes, went out to make sure the gates were all secure. Then I didn't let her stay out very long. I worried that she might start licking the newly treated wood fence and make herself sick.

I did my normal 45 minutes of workout, and went through the rest of my morning routine with the whole sick thing sitting like lead in my stomach. Something about it was so familiar, but exactly what that might be eluded me like smoke in fog. I have had dreams before about my dogs having their paws cut off, even by Greg, who is as unlikely a villain as there ever could be. But I have never seen anything like that before... have I????

So I went to work feeling considerable anxiety, and once I was there, swallowed some Lorazepam and then went through my work day. I was very glad to see my Annie at the door when I got home. And the question still niggles at me... what was THAT all about??

Yesterday I was reading a book called Leaving the Saints, about a woman confronting and forgiving her forgotten memories of abuse in a Mormon family. I have to admit it bothered me. Did that have something to do with it? Her family said she was making it all up. It was all too fantastical to be true, anyway. It was all a bit too close to home. So what do I do with this? I don't think things happen for no reason. Could it just have been a trick of the light? If so, my mind chose how to interpret it. It might have been just overtired imagination. But what an odd thing to imagine. I don't know.... But there you have it. Two sandwiches short of the picnic and half a bubble off plumb, but there you have it.

04.21.2010

Yesterday's "vision" or "delusion" or whatever it was is still hanging over me. I called my counselor to see if he had any time tomorrow or Friday. I don't want to slip backwards. Then, I think it's all a pile of shit. Decide to do better, and you will. Up by the bootstraps. Damn the torpedoes, full speed ahead. Shit.

04.22.2010

    She didn't believe what she was saying
    But saying it, her anger pushed away the pain
    she felt lost and tired
    afraid and alone and trapped
    in world where she didn't belong
    no exit
    no exit
    no exit

04.23.2010

    What I saw was the dark
    pain and death
    the terror in the night
    the blackness of the void
    the nameless formless horror
    of nothingness
    the unbeing of life itself
    Fear become real,
    ever preying on the powerless
    who have given away their strength

    So what is it?
    what is the dark?
    It is whatever it needs to be
    to make you afraid.

05.01.2010

    Somebody just said to me "if you are unhappy with your life, then do what you need to, to change it. And if you aren't willing to do that, then shut up, because nobody wants to hear you complain about it." I didn't know how to respond, so I didn't. It hurt my feelings, and my usual response to hurt feelings is to shut them down and push them away. But let's think about that. Am I unhappy? I'm scared, and I guess that would be considered unhappy. What am I afraid of? Making mistakes. And the fear of making mistakes circles around to the fear of being alone. I will do something wrong, and everyone will leave me. Why am I afraid of being alone? Because if I am alone, I might have to face the darkness that is inside of me? Or the emptiness? I am so good at the dance of denial. Keep dancing. Keep dancing.

Why don't I "just do what I need to do to change it?" What do I need to do to change it? Well, that's the thing, isn't it? The ultimate denial.

05.03.2010

Meeting is today. I hate corporate meetings. Just once, I'd like someone to say what I think - Isn't this the kind of thing that people do, just before they are institutionalized?

Does everybody spend this much time wondering what it all means? Is that why I think it is easier for other people? Because they don't need to find reasons? If I could just be like everybody else, would I be happy? But would I really want to be like them? And could I, if I wanted to? If it doesn't mean anything, then want's the point? Damned if I know.

Author's Note:

A few months later, I decided to quit all the psych meds, change the way I look at the world, and see what happened. What happened was partly scary, partly funny, and mostly good. It turns out that life without the drug companies is not only possible, but survivable.

***

Author's Note:

This was written at a time when I had been off psych drugs for just a couple of months, and was beginning to be able to see things in a different way. Maybe I was not "just wrong." Maybe I was "just different." And maybe, that was okay.

05.29.2010

Christ on a crutch. I always loved that saying, and now as I sit here reading my old poetry, that is what comes to my mind. Maybe there was once a rabbit hole somewhere that I missed falling into in the last fifty years... but I doubt it. I think I hit every sink hole, pit, mine shaft, crater, garbage pile and pavement crack in the continental United States and probably most of the ones in Canada, too. But damned if I'm not still here, and still the funniest person I know. I'm kinda proud of me.

The idea that other people are bipolar and just accept it... could be the greatest idea since sliced bread. Well, homemade bread, because store bought bread is sucky. I wish I had found this stuff years ago. Somebody else is somewhat like me. Not totally like me, because I always remain hyper responsible and don't spend much money. But the mood swings and intensity with which I see the world... somebody else sees it too.

I feel and react and overreact and bounce from one thought to another and the world is ending except that it's not, that was five minutes ago but now it's fine and how are you? I've always felt guilty and wrong about being the way I am, and tried to fix it. I've tried to be like everybody else, even though I'm NOT like everybody else and don't even live on the same planet. I spend about half my time on Zortron. That is MY planet. Okay, I'm not really that delusional. But Zortron is my long standing explanation for why I don't always follow what people are talking about when they are talking about things that bore me and I lose track. Why I walk into so many walls and have been known to apologize to door knobs after bruising myself by failing to avoid them... Why Greg can ask what the traffic is like, and I'll say "clear as a bone..." and it makes sense to me... Why I think things are funny that appall everybody else... I always thought these were symptoms of my wrongness.

Then there are the times when I am fine, and then suddenly not. Suddenly a fog bank comes out of nowhere, and I am sad, and will be sad forever. There is so much pain all around - so many people in pain. Broken treasures cast away.

> The world is such a strange dark place
> I don't know my way and I get lost so easily
> There are rules and I don't know them
> There is a dance and I don't know the steps
> I bleed too easily and I bruise too deep
> I never will belong here

It is all so heavy and so sad. It is sometimes an hour, and sometimes a day, and sometimes weeks.

Sometimes, especially when I am feeling helpless, there is anger. Raging inferno anger that can frighten people if not tightly controlled. It has been a long time since I felt helpless, so I don't feel that so much.

This last year, with all the psych meds, I have lost touch with a good bit of this as everything kind of leveled off into a molasses like slurry of... I don't know... something else. It is like I am finding me all over again, since I have dropped off a drug or two. Perhaps me with more insight. At least I hope so. My biggest fear, now, is anxiety, that seems like an oversized monster that sometimes tries to eat me alive. But I missed the colors in the world, the interest and the energy. I missed me while I was gone.

Excerpt Twenty Two

03.14.2004

So, this has got to be the most stressful day that I have ever had. It all started when my dad woke up. He had been complaining about back pain for about a week now. Today he was actually just lying on the floor. I knew it was serious because my dad never complained about pain. As a matter of fact I only ever saw him cry once, and that was when my brother's friend died of cancer. After hours of telling him he needed to go to the hospital, I finally told him that I was going to call 911. That threat is what did it. So here I am getting my keys and shit together to take him, and the stubborn ass man won't let me drive.

Okay so he gets in his truck and starts driving. I call my mom and her best friend to let them know what is going on and what hospital he was at. I figure I will wait around, get some cleaning done, since I can't do that when my dad was around with his asthma, and wait it out. My dad had to have barely made it to the hospital when I got a frantic call from my mom telling me I needed to get to the hospital now, it was bad.

What the hell I just saw the man. He even drove himself to the hospital. It could not be that bad, could it? I jump in my truck, and fight the tears back. I need to cowgirl up now; I won't do my mom or my dad a lick of good crying. I guess that is just too much to expect from Daddy's little girl. I cried like a baby the whole way there. I was very careful to not speed, because getting pulled over would just take me that much longer to get there. I turn onto the street where the hospital is, the fucking place is in sight, and a damn bike cop starts flashing his lights. How in the hell am I getting pulled over? I did not do anything wrong. I am not going to lie, I did not pull over I kept driving until I was in the parking lot of the hospital. The cop comes up to my window and asks "Do you know why I pulled you over?" What the hell, no, again I did nothing wrong, I just say "No sir." He responded, "Well missy there was someone making a U Turn at the light and you turned in front of them." What the hell kind of law is that when someone making a U Turn has the right of way, that makes absolutely no sense. I just tell him "I am sorry officer I was just focused on getting to the hospital; my dad just had a heart attack." You know how this prick responds to that: "Oh yeah that is not one I have heard before." I did not have time to be shocked because there she was, my savior Deb, my mom's best friend. She runs up and says "Officer, I don't know what she did wrong, but I can tell you she was a little entitled to do so. Her father just had a heart attack and he is in critical condition." WHAT, no one bothered telling me this. ANYWAY the cop let me go; I took my truck to the valet, practically threw my keys at them and ran inside.

There I was greeted by my mom and a doctor. I was told that my dad had what was called a Descending Aorta Aneurism, and he needed surgery immediately. The doctor explained that in all the cases around the world, only 3% of the people lived through this surgery. Not only that, there was about a 97% chance that if he makes it, he would not be able to walk again. Yep, my whole world just came to a standstill. I was only 20. No 20 year old girl is supposed to lose her father. They took us back to see him before they got him into his surgery. Seeing him there, in that condition, was almost more than I could take. He had wires and tubes going out of everywhere. They had put him in a medical coma, but told me to talk to him anyway. You think I would not be so shocked at the sight, having sat at my brother's side for years while he went through his cancer treatments, but that was different. This was my daddy. I took his hand, leaned over and kissed his forehead and told him that everything was going to be okay. He was going to be fine. I told him that I loved him very much, and that he just had to pull through this.

They took him back to prep for surgery and took us back to the private "family room." From there I took my mom's purse and grabbed her phone and walked outside. I had to start making calls. First call was to my aunt Becky, I told her to start calling the rest of the in-state family and I would handle the out-of-state family. I let her know what was going on, and all that I knew. Then I started making my calls, while chain smoking. I tried calling my sister, no answer, so I called her best friend and explained what was going on and that they needed to come now, and prepare for the worst. I called my brother, who was in-state and told him to come now. Then I called my uncle, who had no way of being able to make it. I called my Grandpa, my dad's father. My calls were done. I had another cigarette and went back inside.

This seemed all surreal. I was just smoking a bowl with him the other day. Yes we are a little dysfunctional but it works for us. And now he was hanging on to life by a thread. There was another tower to this hospital, and that is where they took him for the surgery. Family and friends swarmed the hospital. Out of the 50 people in this room, 35 of them where there because of my dad.

Just about when I thought I was going to go absolutely crazy, my older brother walks in. He came up to my mom and I and told the company, "Excuse me guys, I am going to take my girls to get some food and have a cigarette." My mom wanted to stay behind. She put her order in for what she wanted, and my brother and I left. It was going to be another 8 hours of surgery anyway. My dad had already been in there for four. As we stepped into the elevator I finally succumbed to tears. "This is not fair, he has to make it. I know I am being selfish when I say this, but I need my daddy to walk me down the aisle." Like any fantastic big brother, he took me into his arms and said "He will, and if the worst happens I will be there and I will walk you down the aisle on your wedding day." It was comfort, if only a little. Every little girl wants her daddy to walk her down the aisle. No one can replace your dad, no matter how good or bad they are. And mine was awesome.

We had a few cigarettes, got Subway, and came back. I went into the bathroom and wet some paper towels and placed them over my eyes. I was in there for a while, until the red and puffiness was gone. I could not let my mom worry about me at a time like this; she already had enough on her plate. Much against the advice of all the visitors, we did not leave the hospital. It was like I was in some awful nightmare, so surreal. I felt like I was not even there but looking in.

Tick tock, tick tock, tick tock. Seconds turned into minutes and the minutes turned to hours. After what seemed like an eternity of waiting and several false alarms of doctors coming out of the doors to tell the other waiting families what was going on, a doctor came through the door. They called my dad's name and well over half the waiting room stood up.

He had made it through the surgery, but he was far from out of the woods. The hard part was yet to come. He would remain in the medically induced coma for the next day or two and then they would start trying to pull him out, trying being the operative word. The doctors had fought for him the best they could. The rest was up to my dad. The doctor said it was best that we just go home and get some sleep, nothing more could be done now. They would call us if anything changed.

I got into my car and called my sister, updated her on the progress. She said she was on her way, driving. A flight could not get her there any sooner and since she had her husband, the kids, her best friend and grandpa, it was just cheaper. I would see her in the morning, something that I was dreading.

03.15.2004

Oh the dreaded March 15, not an easy day for me as is since this would be the day I lost my baby a while back. Well I woke up today bright and early and left to go pick up my brother. He had let his wife drive him home and his car was still at the hospital.

We got to the hospital waiting room only to find out that, with no surprise, my dad was still in the medically induced coma. I don't remember when, but my sister finally showed up. So of course we let her go back with my mom first, since she had not seen my dad yet. Then my brother and I went back. He looked so weak and helpless. It was difficult to see the machines breathing for him, as well as the tubes that were draining the blood to and from his body.

All in all it was pretty uneventful, but I guess that would be a good thing in this particular situation. We knew the doctors would not wake him up this early, but the good news was that his body was responding well to the surgery. What a weight lifted off all of our shoulders.

03.16.2004

This morning brought wonderful news; they were waking my dad up. What a miracle for him to make it out of surgery, not only that but to be able to wake up. I was so happy. I could not wait to go to the hospital and see him actually responsive.

When I went in there to see him he still had the breathing machine hooked up to him, so he could not talk, but it was great to see his eyes light up when I walked in. I got to his bed side and he immediately started writing to me that he loved me. I cannot tell you what a great feeling that was. As if that was not enough, he can actually move his feet and toes, a good sign that he will be able to walk, with a lot of patience and therapy.

What a wonderful day. My dad beat all the odds and came out victorious. How lucky my family is to get the second chance that many others only dream of. We have this wonderful man in our lives, and that is awesome. He is going to see his grandson, my nephew, who is due in July. Not only that but he will, when the time comes, walk me down the aisle and I will get my daddy daughter dance. How awesome.

10.19.2006

I know, it's bad, I only write when tragedy strikes, but it really is the only time that I need it the most. So here it is - in the last two years I have been married, and now I am getting divorced. Whatever. It was a mistake to marry that man but it is not something I would take back, not for a million dollars. I say this because the man that got a second chance, beat all the odds, and came out shinning in the end, my daddy, got to walk me down the aisle. I got my daddy daughter dance, and cried like a baby in his arms, because I was so close to not getting any of it. So even if I had read the last page first, I would have done it anyway.

That being said, this day has not been a good one, not at all. I woke up today like any other day. I got ready for work, and even though I was running late, I went in and kissed my dad on the cheek, hug him, told him that I loved him, and went off to work.

It was a short shift; I made it home before my mom. I could not shake a bad feeling that I had. There was something not quite right. I could not put my finger on it, but something was seriously wrong. My mom got home around four. We started talking about her friend who had just lost her daughter. I asked her if she had called her lately, and she said no but that she was just about to. Ring, ring, ring…it was the telephone. Chills covered my body; I just knew that this was one phone call we did not want to get.

My dad, while at work, had collapsed in the bathroom and someone found him in there. The emergency response team went straight to work until the ambulance got there. He was in the hospital again, damn it.

The drive there was hell. I kept telling myself that it was going to be okay, he will pull through it. This stupid heart attack was not going to take him; he made it through the impossible already. People have heart attacks every day; some of them don't even know that they are having one. They live and he will too.

I walked into the room; there were those damn machines again. Breathing for him, keeping him alive, he was once again in a medically induced coma. They had to lower his body temperature, something about it helping his heart regulate or whatever I don't know. What I do know is this feels different, wrong.

10.20.2006

To the advice of the doctors and my family, I stayed away. There was nothing that I could do by sitting around in a waiting room. They sent my mom home too, so she could get some rest. She barely pulled into the driveway when they called; he took a turn for the worst.

I was hanging out with my friends when I got the call from my sister in law, "Mary come quick, it's not good."

I was rushed there as fast as we could go. I ran through the parking lot, into the elevator, and to the nurse's desk. "Who are you here to see?" I told her my dad and gave her his name and she said, "Oh you need to come with me now." There he was, with my whole family surrounded by him, the machines breathing for him still.

The doctor told us, well basically, there would be no miracle this time. That now, all that was keeping him alive were the machines. He was brain dead, gone. And we cried.

My mom looked over to me and said, "What do I do?" I know she knew what needed to be done, what my dad wanted. I think she was just asking permission. The whole family knew he did not, for any reason, want to be kept alive by machines. All I could say to her was, "You know what he would want to be done." We called the doctor in and told him we were ready.

He took his breathing tubes out. Then I saw his body struggle for breath. I shook my head. I could not do this. I did not want to watch my daddy die. This is not how I wanted to remember him. I made it out of his room before I collapsed. I was picked up by two nurses who took me to the room next to his. I was having a panic attack. They had to give me an oxygen mask, just for a little bit, but I was lost.

So he is gone, and it is killing me. At least I got the second chance that so many others would give anything for. I got to be walked down the aisle on my wedding day. I got my daddy daughter dance. I got what I had prayed for two years ago. If I only knew that is all I would have gotten I would have been more specific. I would have asked for more. I would have asked for him to grow old. I would have asked for him to be able to see my children. I would have asked for so much more. At least I kissed him the last time I saw him. At least I got to give him one last hug. And THANK GOD at least I told him I love him. I got to tell him I love him one last time, you never think it is the last time when you say that, but at least I don't have to regret not saying it. At least I got to tell him I loved him, and he told me he loved me one last time. At least I got that.

Author's Note:

The funeral was huge. You never know how many people you have touched until your funeral and then you still don't, but your family does. I did stand up and read a poem that I titled "What do you do when your daddy is gone, when you are daddy's little girl." After the funeral when I was walking to my car, some of the guys who worked with my dad when he lead the Emergency Response team at work came up to me and apologized. They had actually been blaming themselves. They said they did everything they could. All I could do is hug them and say that my family and I know that they did everything that they could. We knew that he was their friend. We did not blame them for this in any way; it was just his time to go.

I took from this the memories. Good and bad. I learned to never take for granted what you have. Never leave, even if it's to the store, without telling those you love, that you love them. You never know when it will be the last time you see them.

Excerpt Twenty Three

12.21.2012

So we went to pick up Grandpa in Eastern Idaho today. Mom picked me up at 7 in the morning and I left Ellie with Lisa (my niece) who had stayed the night. Daphne (my step-daughter) was supposed to show up early to help out too.

Along the way I asked my mom what I should get Grandpa for Christmas. She talked about how she didn't even know what to get him. I had tried to shop the night before, thinking of getting some clothes for him, but didn't find anything that looked like he would wear it. After about 3 hours on the road, the weather turned bad and we had snow on the road. We weren't expecting snow probably because we hadn't had any back at home for so long. It's been quite a dry year. I asked Mom if she looked at the weather report before we left and she said she didn't even think of it. I said, "If I had known we could have brought the pickup for 4 wheel drive and chains." I really hoped it wouldn't be too bad.

We slowed way down and noticed some car speed past us probably still going 75 mph. A little ways up the car in front of us hit the brakes suddenly and we had a scare since it was so slick. I noticed the dumb reason everyone hit the brakes on the snowy road; the car that sped past us had just spun and slid off the side of the freeway.

We kept on going slowly but Mom had to call and let Grandpa know we'd be a little late. It was then I found out he wanted to take us to lunch at the senior center, so mom said that we would just have to meet him there. I asked Mom why she didn't tell me earlier we were having lunch at the senior center and she replied like a kid in trouble. "He really wants to take us there." I asked why but not really towards her but she replied, "Probably to show us off to his friends." She added that with the snow we will probably miss lunch anyways so not to worry about it. Even though we had to slow down, we still unfortunately, were not that late.

When we got there we found him in the corner playing solitaire on an ancient computer. The screen was huge and took up the whole width of the desk. Fitting for this place I thought. He was drinking a Pepsi and said, "Well go sign in."

We walked back to the door and the ladies sitting there behind a table showed us where to sign in. We walked back over to him and waited a while as he considered his next move and sipped his drink. Finally, after what seemed like forever, he got up from his game to go show us to our seats. He introduced us to a couple of people. He showed us the four seats he saved; I wasn't sure why there were four but didn't question it. He is hard of hearing nowadays and I know it's easier to not ask questions unless I have to.

Then some lady who was younger than him came over and gave him a gift at the spot he was standing by, so I assumed that was his seat. He talked with her for a bit and I couldn't help but think that this lady might be a little more than a friend. Mom was standing next to him so when he was done with his conversation, he looked at me and he pointed out for me to go to the other side of the table. I would need to go around the long table to the end of the room just to get to the other side to sit across from her.

There were like ten 8-foot tables all put together end to end from the front of the room to almost the back. My grandpa walked away soon after, probably to finish his solitaire game. The people around us struck up short conversations about where we were from and the weather. Typical old people conversation... I really don't normally mind hanging out with older people and was surprised at my lack of patience with these ones.

I decided to sit down and the lady behind Mom motions to me that I was sitting in the wrong seat so I agreed to move over one. Then the guy who was sitting next to Grandpa's chair said I was in the wrong seat. I told him politely, "My grandpa said he saved two seats on this side and that lady told me I was in the wrong spot in the other chair." So then he replied, "Well, you can sit there but this spot is saved then." He leaned over in the spot across from his and put a spoon in a cup. I looked around realizing that's how they saved seats. Grandpa had saved the four he pointed out so I was confused and a little concerned I might be upsetting the old folks for taking spots they wanted to save for their friends but might not have marked just yet. The guy told me he was saving it for his sister. No one ever did sit in the first spot I sat down in (the fourth seat saved by Grandpa).

Grandpa came back over just before noon and sat down with us. As seniors started to stream in he started pointing out some facts about them to us. He would point and say, "That lady is Susie and she is nice," Or, "That lady is my friend Lucy." A little bit later he pointed out a lady behind me and said, "Do you see her in the fur coat? The one right there, at the table next to us…" Then when we acknowledged we saw her he said, "Her husband died about 6 months ago." I thought oh how sad as he says "She's looking pretty good now!" Oh God! Please, I do not need to hear this.

I started to realize that everyone he pointed out and commented about were women. Ugh! I understand that when people get old they do not die yet. They still have the same basic needs and desires that we all have. However, my grandpa cheated on my grandmother! He left his wife with 7 kids for another woman! He was married more times than I could remember! My mom told me stories about how in junior high there were rumors that her dad knocked up the neighbor lady and that she was pregnant with his baby and not her own husband's. Then Grandmother confirmed his ways, a time or two, with her own stories; some about other husbands asking her to control her husband and to get him to stop going after their wives and how frustrated and hurt she felt because she couldn't control her "loving" husband.

Anyways some ladies were walking around with a cart filling up glasses with apple juice. She came to me and asked if I wanted some and I said "no thanks." She said, "Are you sure?" I said yes and that I didn't need it. Quite honestly, the thought of having apple juice at the senior center just grossed me out. I told her I would drink water. She refilled the water pitcher for me.

Someone came in during this time and left a bunch of bakery items in the back on some tables. Grandpa jumped up and left the table fast! I didn't think he could move so fast in fact. Then I noticed everyone else was too! It was a mad dash over there and I couldn't quite tell what was going on. He came back over with a loaf of bread and asked Mom if she liked that kind. She said "yes." He walked over to the coat room and put it under his cowboy hat, along with his coat. I noticed everyone was doing the same, quickly putting their bakery items in purses or under hats or hiding them in their coats. As Grandpa came to sit down again, a lady came up to show off what she snagged - a pie! Grandpa was jealous. He said "Oooh, how did you get that one?" She said "the same way you did last week. I was there first!" They laughed over that for a little bit in a flirty way.

Finally the noon hour came and a lady started walking up to the microphone up in front of the long tables. She started talking but wasn't standing close enough for anyone to hear, so the old folks started to yell "talk into the microphone!" Someone else understood the situation and went up to show her how to talk into it. She started over, welcoming everyone to lunch as the crowd calmed down again.

Meanwhile, some guys walked in late and came behind Grandpa and started talking loudly to him so I have no idea what else the lady up front said. I tried to hear her as I was nervous about the whole situation and felt very out of place. Having lunch at the senior center was already thus far nerve wracking as I learned the ropes of lunch time behaviors. Then I heard Grandpa introducing Mom and I so I turned and acknowledged the guys. They were shaking our hands and loudly telling us "It's so good to meet you."

Just then everyone was standing up, with the exception of the lady next to me. I asked Mom what to do and she said they were standing for the pledge of allegiance, so we stood and said it. Then we got to sit back down and they did some announcements and what not, and then another lady came up to the microphone. She said she really wanted to tell a Christmas story. She started off about a little boy and his red wagon, but that was all I got to hear as grandpa's cell phone started ringing loudly! It was like an old fashioned telephone ring – the ear piercing BLLRRRRING BBLLLRRRRIIINGGG!!!! AND he answered it. He had the thing turned on so loud we could hear the person on the other end.

Grandpa told him (on the other end) that he was at lunch but they continued their conversation anyways. He kept saying, "What?" but even I could hear what the guy was saying on the other end. People started to glare at Grandpa, and then Mom started saying "Dad! Take the call outside or go in another room! Dad!" She was very unsuccessful in trying to get Grandpa to either walk away or end the call. I didn't know whether to laugh or hide. It went on, this little old lady's story, as she seemed so unaware of the chaos going on with us at our end of the room.

Mom kept trying to get Grandpa to leave the room or hang up and Grandpa was still trying to hear the guy on the other end of the phone. Finally Mom made some headway with him. She said whispering very loudly "Dad! Take it off speaker phone!" At that point he pulled the phone away from his ear to look at it and see if he could figure out how to turn down the volume. Mom took the opportunity to also see about quieting the call. But really, I think the phone was just that loud! He probably bought the thing at some "cell phones for seniors" store where they come standard with volume that is ungodly loud and huge buttons they can see. Anyways, they couldn't figure out how to turn down the volume I guess, or they just gave up trying, and Grandpa put it back up to his ear. At this point he understood that he needed to end the call, as it sounded like he was trying to wrap it up with a bunch of "uh huh, yep" and "ok"s. Finally he finished the conversation. Let me tell you, it was such a relief! And then the lady up front thanked everyone for listening to her story and wished us all a Merry Christmas.

Grandpa stood up and walked to the front of the room. I asked mom where he was headed. She said he had to help pass out the food. "Oh," I say. Next someone said a prayer and then said that the lunch would now be served to us. "Yay!" I thought. But who is this lady running to the front of the room yelling "Wait!" She yells again, "Wait! We forgot to do the drawing!" The other lady said into the microphone, "Oh yes! We almost forgot about the drawing!" She said some spiel about Sam's Club and how you can get a membership here at the senior center today. Then she thanked them for coming and telling us all about it. The Sam's Club lady held out a bowl for the drawing and asked the speaker lady to draw a name. She did and said, "Our winner of the cute snowman display of goodies is...<insert long pause as she shuffles

the names in the bowl>...Kate!" There is an audible exhale throughout the crowd as we all wait to see who this Kate is.

I am thinking there is another Kate in the room as Mom and I didn't enter this drawing. But as we wait, I start to feel a little nervous. She calls the name again, "Kate?" I look at Mom as she is sitting there looking so uncomfortably. I ask quietly, "Mom? Did you enter a drawing?" She is sitting there not saying anything with this nervous grin on her face. I start to get a sinking feeling in my stomach as I'm not sure what to do. I am positive my mom doesn't know either. The speaker asks again, "Kate A.!? Please come forward to claim your prize!" At this point, I am pretty sure it is my mother who won and I look at Mom and say under my breath "I think it is you Mom!" Then I can hear Grandpa up front yelling, "That's my daughter! Yes! Kate, come on up! Where is she?" I turn and look at Mom, and she still has that nervous grin on her face. She sheepishly starts to raise her hand half way up.

Grandpa brings the prize to Mom and yells "Kate! Why didn't you come up there? You won!" He hands her this huge clear gift bag with stacking boxes inside painted like a snowman, complete with fabric scarf, gloves and hat. It is about 3 feet tall. I promptly told Grandpa, "Well how was she supposed to know there wasn't another Kate here? And we didn't even enter the drawing." He said, "Yeah, I did it for you guys." He walked back up front proudly to get ready to deliver food trays.

Someone leaned over and asked Mom what she was going to do with the basket she won. She said laughing nervously, "We'll probably give it to my dad, Bob." We got our food a few minutes later. It was surprisingly good. Ham, baked potato, white rolls, mixed vegetables, carrot cake with cream cheese frosting and some kind of Jello salad. We ate peacefully and made some small talk with the people around us.

This whole time Mom kept worrying about 'Seymour' my brother's carnivorous plant, (yes she actually named the freakin' plant!). She had brought it to drop off at my aunt's house on our way back through another town. She actually mentioned it several times before and during lunch, "I am worried about Seymour. Maybe you should go check on him." So finally I paused during eating and ran out to the car to go get the plant and bring it in so it wouldn't freeze to death. It's a tropical plant so I too was worried it wouldn't last that long in the car, but I also didn't expect to be stuck in the senior center for hours.

When I was finished filling my stomach with more food, I noticed the routine of people taking their trays to the front. There was a table set up with buckets full of water and a trash can for scraps next to it. There were small wood boards attached to each bucket with a spoon, a fork and a knife on them to identify which bucket to put each utensil in.

I waited a little bit but Mom and Grandpa weren't done yet, so then I decided to just go put my tray away. As I was up there, two different people said to me, "Now where are you from?" I said "Boise." One of them continued and said that my grandpa probably rigged the drawing. I had no idea how to respond, so I just dismissed it and laughed at the "joke." Then I tried to make my way back down the aisle but there were a lot of slow people walking and also some standing in the aisle talking. Another lady leaned over and asked me how my grandpa rigged the drawing. I just laughed it off and again mentioned how funny it was that my mom won. She wasn't done and asked what we were planning on doing with the basket. I said probably give it to Grandpa for Christmas.

I finally get back to my seat and Mom asked me to take her and Grandpa's trays to the front. I heard another lady come over to Mom and ask what she is going to do with her prize. She responds,

"Well it looks like there are many goodies inside so probably share it with the family over Christmas." She mentioned her grandkids and that her dad was coming home with us. The lady just said "humph" and left her alone. As I came back to the table the second time after cleaning the trays, Mom was clearing the table.

A lady who sat near me gave me a stack of trays from her group and said something about me being younger and more able. So I took their trays to the front too. As I came back again my mom said to hurry up and help clear the tables. It was obvious that someone else said something to her again. We started taking the butter and sour cream dishes, as well as the water pitchers, to the front of the tables. People started leaving just as quickly as they came in.

I sat down to wait for Grandpa as I didn't know what else to do then. I noticed the lady next to me was still sitting there. She asked me if I knew where her brother was. I looked around and thought that was him in the coat room. I said, "I think he is over there getting his coat." She said, "Well I can't get up." I asked, "Do you need help?" She said "yes." So I asked how she needed me to help her as I grabbed her arm to maybe just assist her standing up. She said with a sly tone, "Oh no, you need to lift me." When she saw my confusion she said, "Under my arms. Lift me under my arms so I can stand up straight!" "Ok," I said. So I tried hard to lift her but I couldn't get her up. I thought I was going to break my "young and able" back.

I let go and she said, "Oh, so not as strong as you thought, huh?" very sarcastically. I got mad then. I am one who is usually up for a challenge and when challenged I take the problem head on! So I asked her, "Exactly how would you like me to help you." So she said that she would help me too by using the chairs next to her to lift with her arms. I got her up that time. I can't even remember if she had thanked me at that point. But then I asked her if she needed help with her coat; anything to get her out of there faster while I waited on my grandpa. Of course she said yes. I took it off the back of her chair to hand it to her, but she put her arm out like she needed me to dress her. I put it on her left arm and then she couldn't stretch her right arm out for the other sleeve, so I had to wrap it around her and stretch the coat to get her arm in it. Then her brother came over and said, "Oh, I see you managed without me." They walked away and left.

Grandpa came over after and asked if we were ready? Mom asked him where he was parked since we would need to follow him. She reminded him she didn't know how to get to his house. So we walked out together with me following behind. Unfortunately, since I was last, I felt I needed to hold the door for the next person but the next person wasn't as courteous. So I sat there holding the door for the rest of the crowd which didn't stop streaming out for a few minutes and none of them offered to take the door from me. They didn't even thank me! By then, I had lost sight of my grandpa and my mom. I saw that 3 inches of snow had fallen since we were inside, and thought we have to drive back to Boise in this shit!

I made my way to the car where I found my mom looking for an ice scraper. I just got in and started the car to get it warm. We resituated Seymour in the back seat and tried to get most of the snow off the car without a scraper. I asked where Grandpa was and Mom didn't quite know. The back window was covered with snow and fogged up so I was nervous about backing out so soon.

Then we saw Grandpa's car pulling out onto the street from its parking spot along the sidewalk. Mom said, "There he is, follow him." We jumped in and I pulled out from our parking spot across the street, but I was facing the wrong direction because of the way the parking spots were laid out. As I was headed to turn around at the intersection, we saw Grandpa stopping at the stop sign in the opposite direction. I waited until it was safe to turn around so we could follow him but he was gone.

I asked Mom, since she was in the passenger seat, where he went but she said she didn't know. "How could you not know Mom? You should have been looking," I said. We got to the stop sign after having to pause for some other cars and the senior bus. We didn't see him, so we turned left to look for him near the highway. We spotted him at a stop sign a few blocks away and caught up to him. As we were slowing down, we started to slide and I realized we were going to slide through the stop sign onto the highway. Luckily I didn't see anyone coming too closely as we drove right onto the highway following Grandpa.

I saw him turning onto a side street to the left. As we followed him, Mom said, "Now when we get there, we will both go into the bathroom and look around at his toiletries to see what he uses. Then we will have an idea of what to get him for Christmas." Wonderful, I thought, snooping through Grandpa's bathroom. When we got to his house, he showed off some things on his table. He asked if I liked a necklace he made with a polished rock in it and I said quickly, "Sure, yeah." He said, "Ok and what about this for Karissa?" He held up a very pretty silver necklace with a small blue polished rock and I was jealous. He always cared about Karissa more than me or my brother. I said, "Yeah she will love it!" He then asked if John would like a belt buckle and I said, "No, probably not Grandpa. He doesn't wear belts." Grandpa said, "Oh, well, I don't have anything for him." I said, "Well he is the kind of guy who doesn't care if he gets something or not." John really wouldn't care. Grandpa looked discouraged and looked around the table but didn't find anything else. He packed up the necklaces and got some other stuff together.

Mom said she was going to use the bathroom and left us, so I looked around the junk in his living room. He has stuff stacked everywhere in his little tiny trailer. He continued to tidy up and then Mom came out giving me the look that it was my turn. I went in and actually had to pee, so I did. But as I sat there on the pot, I realized that he has a floral fluffy shower curtain, a pink scale and fake flowers in a vase, all in his bathroom. I couldn't help but wonder if they were various things from his many women, collected after break ups or divorces. When I was done, I searched quickly and noticed only dollar store type things. It was then I figured whatever I got him he would be happy with. When I came out, they were ready to go.

It was still snowing so Mom designated me to drive again. As I started to pull out to turn around in the driveway/yard, Grandpa yelled to gun it. I kinda laughed wondering why he would say that. Knowing why I would question Grandpas comment, my mom said, "Yes! You will need to step on it to get out of here with all the snow on the rocks." I didn't really "gun it," but we got out of there fine. I thought we had driven down his road quite a ways to get back to the road we turned from, but as we approached the first intersection Grandpa said, "Turn here!" I didn't really have time but tried and we almost ended up in the ditch on the corner. I wasn't sure why he thought I would know where I was going.

He directed me to follow the road for quite a ways until we hit the highway and then I knew where to go. He started to point out houses of people he knew who used to live wherever. I didn't listen too much since most of them had to do with people I didn't know. We drove for almost an hour to the next town and made a stop at my aunt's work to give her Seymour.

As we left, Grandpa mentioned that she has lost some weight. Funny, I didn't even notice but he probably doesn't ever see her. Actually, the last time would have been at Grandmother's funeral. I still can't believe he came... I guess it might have been more for their kids, but they are grown-ups, so who knows.

As we pulled away, Grandpa said he doesn't know why she (my aunt) doesn't talk to him. I thought this was strange, as he talked, because she says the same thing about him. She thinks that it's because he doesn't claim her as his child. He assumed Grandmother was fooling around, just as he was, around the time my aunt was conceived and born. I am not sure how much of what I hear has been truthful or really what is the truth. All I know is that he hasn't been involved much in my life. But I do believe what my grandmother told me and she said she was never unfaithful to him. I saw an article a few years ago in his local paper stating he was "Senior of the Month," and when asked how many kids he had, he only said five. The whole family wondered who the two were that he didn't claim.

Next he pointed out a bar and said, "There's the old 33 Club." Now this wouldn't bother me, but he is freaking going back to the church like he has never done anything wrong. I know it is not for me to judge but really??? Can you cheat on your wife and go to the bars drinking and sleeping around and then when you get old decide that since you are old it's time to pray and become religious? The more I think about it, I think the church couldn't have ever known of his ways because he would have been excommunicated and would not be volunteering in the temple now. UGH! He makes me really angry.

He continued talking for quite a while. He would talk about houses we drove by and how so and so had a get together and when. Or those ladies that used to live in that house used to be so nice and he never knew what happened to them. He talked to my mom about his life insurance, or money in stocks or something, that he had her named as the beneficiary. He wanted her to know so that when he died she would know to look for it and she would have money to bury him. It was a little sad.

Oh and he talked about my uncle who died unexpectedly three months after Grandmother did. He asked Mom if she found out why he died and she said, "No, did you?" He said "no." She said she didn't want to pay all the money just to find out why. He said he didn't want to know because if it was due to drugs, he doesn't know how he would live with himself. I don't feel that there is a difference and really we should know. No matter what, the outcome is the same. Since losing Grandmother to cancer, I would like to know what the heck he died of too to make sure it isn't a genetic or hereditary trait.

We passed one place and Grandpa started talking about a couple who used to live there. He mentioned that they had some of the best parties. He told us a story about one of them. The husband started looking for his wife and he couldn't find her, or Grandpa. The husband must have assumed they (his wife and Grandpa) were "getting it on" outside in the car. Grandpa talked about how funny it was when the party goers finally came downstairs to see them playing pool in the basement. He was surprised the husband actually thought that he (Grandpa) would be "getting it on with his wife." He said they were just playing pool the whole time and didn't know why no one ever looked there when they were missing. Grandpa said he always had great relationship with the wife.

I tried to tune out. It was strange to hear my grandpa talk about sex by saying "getting it on" and not just once in his story, but several times! AND this is not an image I want to have or think about my grandpa "getting it on!" I am sure that he WAS "getting it on" in the car outside. OR he had been "getting it on" with her enough in the past, that they all assumed that is what the wife and Grandpa were doing. THAT wouldn't surprise me but I don't really want to hear about it from my 85 year old grandpa!

We drove beyond American Falls and my grandpa talked about my grandmother's property and my great grandfather. I wish I knew more and I really miss my grandmother. He said he heard that the farmer who bought the land plowed it so that he only removed the sagebrush and not the wild grass. He said he didn't know such a technique existed. (He heard it from another aunt so who knows how accurate that is since she is a compulsive liar). I said I didn't know either.

My heart aches so badly that we lost not only Grandmother but also her parents' homestead. I really hope the new owner doesn't tear the houses down. I want to meet the guy to talk to him about it all. I really would like to go take the rest of her stuff out of the old house, and possibly take wood if he is going to tear the house down (or burn it). I tried hard not to cry as we passed the area. But really this time last year, I NEVER would have imagined we'd be picking up Grandpa for Christmas! We would have been picking up Grandmother instead!

It makes me angry that she had to die before him. Aren't women supposed to live longer than men? And why would God take her from us and not this asshole who thinks he is my grandpa. He was never around for anything anyways. I am so angry and deeply hurt. I loved my grandmother so much! I just always thought I would have more time to spend with her. I should have visited more. I just really thought she would be around forever, as unreal as that is to think. Great Grandmother was so strong and lived on her own until 94, so I thought we had another 14 years or so. I still remember her out there on the ranch replacing fence posts. I just thought Grandmother would be too. I am mad that she had to die the way she did too. It was fast looking back, but at the time it felt very slow and horrible.

December 29th

Well the rest of Grandpa's visit went without much drama. I ended up buying him a huge package of mixed nuts from Costco. He wanted to buy it for himself 'til he saw the price, so I grabbed it, wrapped it up and gave it to him. I did notice on Christmas he mentioned he felt bad that he didn't have gifts for everyone and I actually felt bad for him. The only reason he was with us was because the rest of his living five kids didn't invite him to their Christmas. Somehow Mom accidentally did. She mentioned to him that it was a shame he couldn't come visit her so he said he could. But then he later called and said he couldn't find a ride. So Mom volunteered to go get him because she felt bad for him. No one wants him around for Christmas because of what he has done. I think he dug his grave and is laying in it!

When I told Mom that John and I were going to Utah to see my other grandparents after Christmas, she said that Grandpa had no way home. I said we could probably swing him by his house along the way. It would put us out a couple hours of driving but easier than my mom taking a day off work, driving by herself and going there and back in one day. John, for some odd reason, likes Grandpa and didn't see any problem driving him home. We told Grandpa we wanted to leave early the day after Christmas, which was fine with him.

We took the pickup so there was room for all of us plus Grandpa. I really didn't want to sit bitch in the front, so I told Robby to sit up there in the middle with his dad and Grandpa. Me and the girls would sit in the back and it gave me the space I needed away from him.

I didn't hear much from him since the pickup isn't exactly quiet, which really was fine with me. When we got to his house, I needed to use the bathroom and noticed his water wouldn't come on. He was showing everyone around, showing the kids rocks and telling them about the rocks' names and where he found them. He talked about his shop and that if we had more time he could take us out there to show us. He showed John and the kids a picture frame with about twelve rocks in it and explained that some of them were fossilized dinosaur poop. Ellie was excited about that one! He gave it to me to take home. It was covered with a thick layer of dust so he tried to dust it off before I took it.

I told him his water wouldn't come on and that I was nervous that his pipes froze while he was gone. He disappeared for a while to fix it, and came back about 10 minutes later. John and I are not sure how he fixed it but he showed us it worked and we didn't ask. Grandpa seemed ready for us to go by then. And we were anxious to get going too since we still had another 2 hours of driving to go.

In the pickup, the kids asked if I would be throwing Grandpa's rocks away. I was shocked and I got pretty mad about it. I felt very possessive about them by then and thought this might be one of the only things I will ever get of my grandpa's. I treasure them as ugly as it might be. He spends a lot of time hunting for the rocks and then bringing them home in buckets to spend even more time polishing them up. I am feeling more emotional about it, probably because I miss my grandma so much. I hung the frame on the wall in my bedroom, on a nail that was already there. Next to that, I took great care hanging the picture canvas I had made over Christmas, of Great Grandmother's homestead house. I made sure the picture of the house is above Great Grandmothers chair. I am starting to get quite the collection going.

Excerpt Twenty Four

09.19.2010

I thought we might go camping this week. I was looking forward to soaking up some tranquility out in the Owyhees. Alas, it was not to be. My husband's cousin Joe had said he was coming to drop off a car with us "on the 18th," but had not said a word in the last couple of weeks. I was hoping he had decided against it. Rob is great at fixing cars, but I'd rather he didn't do it when he is supposed to be out camping with me. I especially didn't want him to fix cousin Joe's car, because (a) the problems with cousin Joe's car are ghostlike and transient, which sounds like a lot of problem chasing, (b) cousin Joe's car is a "classic" old project, which means that it is a time, money and energy pit, (c) we don't have room in our driveway for another car, and (d) cousin Joe plans to leave it here UNTIL NEXT APRIL. This means a whole winter outside. The car is a convertible. I don't want to be blamed when that snowy white interior is soggy and smelling of mildew.

But cousin Joe emailed Friday night, and said he'd be here around four in the afternoon, with his convertible and his new wife. We spent a good part of Saturday cleaning house and shampooing carpets, so our dog resident home would be suitable for company. Joe was true to his word, and showed up around 5:30. He took us out for pizza. He really is a nice man, and his new wife is very sweet. The car turned out to look like the mutant offspring of a nuclear submarine, and something very white and ugly. Rob cooed over it, I think mainly because that is the polite thing to do when a car guy shows his uglimobile to another car guy. Over pizza, Joe announced that he and Martha would be getting up and leaving first thing, so they could get back to

Nevada. I perked up, thinking that we could see them off, load our quads, and at least have all Sunday to ride. That, alas, was also not to be.

Daisy, our ninety pound baby girl greyhound mix, was ecstatic over Joe and Martha. When Joe sat down on the couch, she tried to climb on top of him and sit on his head. When they went to bed, she shoved open their bedroom door and then jumped on top of them. She was VERY happy.

This morning dawned, all bright and well, sort of cloudy. I noticed first thing that Daisy's water bowl was completely empty, which is unusual. It's a big bowl, and usually it is still half full when I dump it out and give her fresh water in the morning. Martha was in the shower when I chanced into our back storage room, which is right next to the second bathroom. The floor was covered with a shimmering liquid sheen. I told Rob that I had found out where all the water had gone; Lake Daisy was filling the storage room. He took a look, and announced that it was not Lake Daisy at all. It was coming from the bathroom.

We mopped up most of it while Martha was still showering, so we could not track down where it was coming from. Rob started theorizing about the shower leaking, which was a truly nasty thought. Daisy, in the meantime, had been laying in the dining room happily chewing on her rear end. She jumped up, leaving behind a nasty looking string of brown liquid on our freshly shampooed carpet. The smell was indescribable. Rob said it was the "contents of impacted anal glands." Since Rob knew what it was, I thought it only fair that he should clean it up. It left a big spot on the freshly shampooed carpet.

He had just finished when Martha, who had just emigrated from Columbia, came out of the bathroom exclaiming in her somewhat halting English that she hadn't used the toilet. She kept saying it over and over. The toilet was, in fact, the source of all the water. It was pouring out from the under the base. Cousin Joe tried to turn off the valve, but it stuck. Rob tried, and the handle broke, but the flood came to a temporary halt, so we took Joe and Martha out for doughnuts, and saw them off.

Home Depot has a whole section labeled "toilet." It seems that toilets are amazingly complex and full of parts. Rob bought a valve, and a nasty looking thing called a "Toilet Bowl Gasket." I wondered how he knew so much about toilets.

We went home, and turned off power to the water pump, and then Rob told me to turn on the kitchen sink to bleed down the pressure. I turned on the water without thinking about it. He saw the steam coming out of the sink, and somewhat impolitely asked me WHY I had turned on the hot water. It turns out you don't want to drain the hot water tank with the water pump off, or something bad could happen and you could burn out the elements in your hot water tank. Oops. I turned off the hot water, turned on the cold water, and took up position as assistant toilet fixer.

Rob took the little pipey thingy off the valve and took the valve out of the wall. He quickly replaced it. So far, so good. He undid the toilet bolts and pulled the whole toilet out of the floor. Under it was a rather nasty looking hole with disgusting looking brown goo around it. He pulled out the ring of brown goo and replaced it with the "Toilet Bowl Gasket," which is another ring of brown goo. He dropped the toilet back over the hole, and bolted it back down after swearing about the fact that the previous owner had done it wrong. There were some little round washer thingies that should have been on the toilet, but instead were shoved up into the caps. The caps were full of goo, which he cleaned out.

Then, the pipe thingy where the water goes in fell off the back of the toilet. Rob swore some more about that, and commented that that might have been part of the water problem as well. He put it back on, and then turned on the water. That is when the tank started to leak. Rob swore even more, turned the water off, and tightened whatever it is that you tighten to firmly attach the tank to the toilet. He speculated about how so much stuff could have suddenly and simultaneously come loose at the same time. Some of the speculation had to do with the fact that cousin Joe weighs maybe three hundred pounds. He finished tightening things and turned the water back on. Nothing leaked.

He flushed the toilet. Water immediately came gushing out from underneath it. Rob swore some more. We went back to Home Depot to buy another "Toilet Bowl Gasket." We had bought a "NO-SEEP NO. 3." It turns out there are others. We bought another one with a box that proclaimed "NO-SEEP NO. 10! 40% MORE WAX! For problem areas that need EXTRA THICK wax! Faster installation! More positive seal!" Which led me to wonder... how are you supposed to tell if you have a problem toilet? Why would you have wanted to buy a Toilet Bowl Gasket with slower installation and less positive seal in the first place?

We went home and Rob pulled the toilet out of the floor again. He put in the "NO-SEEP NO. 10 Toilet Bowl Gasket." He put the toilet back where it belonged, and turned the water back on. I began to intone a prayer to the Toilet Bowl God:

O Great God of the Toilet Bowls!
Hear our prayer!
Bless this toilet that it may leak no more!
We shall evermore bring you offerings.

That is where Rob told me to shut up. He flushed the toilet. It did not leak. Since my prayer to the Great God of the Toilet Bowls had obviously been heard, I finished my devotional. Rob laughed. We cleaned up the mess, but it was now almost noon, so after re-shampooing the carpet, we decided to just get groceries, watch a movie, and order pizza for dinner. And that is what we did this weekend.

Excerpt Twenty Five

Ahh, the life of a trucker. Freedom, adventure, the romance of the open road. Truckers have it made, getting paid to travel, sitting high above the traffic; they are carefree gypsies of the American highways.

By one o'clock in the afternoon, I've been blissfully slumbering for seven hours, except for a few small interruptions:

7:30 a.m. Dale's alarm clock goes off.

9:30 a.m. Talk radio infiltrates my formerly sleeping brain with the current national crisis. After I yell at him, Dale turns it down.

10:00 a.m. Dale arrives at the consignee. The truck stops moving and I wake up.

10:05 a.m. Having lowered the landing gear on the rear trailer, Dale pulls forward and drops it. Then he drops the dolly (that little 800 pound piece of metal that connects the trailers. It is also useful for smashing fingers, crushing limbs, and causing normally mild mannered truckers to curse fluently).

10:15 a.m. He backs the remaining trailer on to the dock. This causes a minor jolt reminiscent of 50,000 pounds of truck hitting a concrete dock. At slow speed, of course. haha

10:20 a.m. The forklift begins unloading the trailer. Imagine trying to sleep while a small elephant keeps jumping on the bed.

10:50 a.m. They finish unloading the first trailer. Dale pulls forward, drops that trailer, hooks the dolly and drops it in front of that trailer, hooks the other trailer, and puts it on the dock. The elephant comes back.

http://www.thesecretlivesofpeople.com

11:35 a.m. Dale moves the second trailer to another dock, so that the loading elephant can get started. By the time both trailers are loaded and hooked, it's about 12:30.

By 1:15, bright-eyed and bursting with energy, I sit up on the edge of the bunk and get breakfast, which involves pouring cornflakes into a plastic bowl, dumping sugar on them, and then discovering that there are two tablespoons of milk left. What an adventure!

By 3:00, we're in heavy traffic and I'm glad I'm not driving. Dale is doing a masterful job at avoiding collision with the erratically darting, mindless automobiles that make up Bay Area traffic.

I'm doing a not so masterful job of trying to read. It's a lost cause. This particular road could be used to torture test tanks. Dale is back to listening to talk radio. DOOM! DOOM! We're all DOOMED!!! I give up and decide to contemplate fingernail dirt. I've been in the truck since 6 am, when I went in to the rest area at Dunnigan.

At 6:30, we stop at the truck stop in Corning to buy a loaf of bread, get a shower, and grab dinner from the deli - fried chicken, Jello, and raspberry iced tea. The fried chicken was cooked in 1987 and reheated this morning.

I drive out from Corning. Thirty miles down the road is Redding, a small town where children are taught starting in grade school that "merge" means "aim for the duals." Even at 2:00 a.m., when there is no traffic, one dedicated Reddingite will be lurking at the top of an on ramp waiting for a truck. You can slow down, speed up, it doesn't matter. They will match speeds and aim for the duals.

Past Redding, traffic is almost always light up into Dunsmuir Canyon. I5 here is twisty and hilly, but unless we're loaded heavy, this is a relaxing stretch of road to soak up window time. If we are loaded heavy, this is a great place to practice shifting gears until your leg falls off. Our truck has thirteen forward gears, and every once in a while, I'll lose track. "Uh.... 6th direct, yeah, it was (grind)... No, 7th direct (grind) NO, NO! 6th OVER! That's it! Someone once told me there are two kinds of truckers - those who get lost in their transmissions every once in a while, and those who lie.

Just past the California - Oregon border is the Siskiyou Summit, the top of a long steep grade that goes down into Ashland. In the winter, the mile over the top of this grade is a favorite place for automobile drivers who think that tire chains are kinky marital aids, and truckers who don't want to chain up, to run into each other. This is always a happy occasion, that other truckers celebrate by making colorful comments on their CBs, while the fun loving four wheelers try to dodge around the trucks and beat them to the accident site, where they can try to run into MORE trucks, and as an extra bonus, exchange friendly finger gestures with each other and those carefree gypsy truckers. I love winter in a truck.

Excerpt Twenty Six

I wonder if your life makes you crazy, or if being crazy blesses you with a crazy life. When I was a kid my big brother Bill knew everything, and had done everything. I wanted to be like that, and have stories to tell. Mind you, I don't remember any of Billie's stories - just an impression that he had them. He had been in the Navy, had friends who died in airplane crashes, had driven the Alcan, and fixed cars, worked on road construction, and impressed his little sister, who was 16 years his junior. It took me thirty years to catch up to him.

Remember when thirty was "old?" I do. But my first thirty years, while being somewhat unpleasant, were not all that interesting. Being a kid sucked, but that only takes you so far on the interesting scale. Besides, with years of therapy, I have gone over that ground so many times that the landmarks are all boringly familiar, even if some of them are still painful. Being married at 16 and having a child at 18, well, that was a mixed bag. Some parts good, some bad, some very bad. High school dropout, good Mormon housewife, church librarian, part time grocery store clerk, part time housekeeper. I cooked, canned, cleaned and kept garden with the best of them, and enjoyed some of it. I still miss the peculiar satisfaction that comes from having a pantry full of a couple of hundred jars of food you canned yourself. I don't miss marching on the party line, and being chastised for being politically incorrect. I was politically incorrect all the time.

How easy is it to be politically incorrect when you are a good Mormon housewife? Let me illustrate. My father in law fell off of a kitchen stool. He had been drinking at the time, but he was not Mormon, so that was okay. While on the way to the floor, he hit his head on the breakfast bar. How's that for an embarrassing way to injure your spinal cord? We held vigil at the hospital all day, which is exhausting. My husband, my mother in law, sister in law, and me, all waiting for someone to tell us how to feel about tomorrow.

Late in the day, I committed a major transgression. We had finally received news that Ken was being moved into a room on the second floor, and while it appeared that he may have lost some function in his right arm, and it was unclear whether he would regain it, he was otherwise going to be okay. We retreated to the second floor, where the only seating was in an unused hallway just down from Ken's soon to be room. There was one chair short, so everyone sat down, except me. But I was wearing jeans and a t-shirt, and feeling pretty casual at the time, so I sat down on the floor, with my back against the wall. My good Mormon husband came unglued. Apparently the Doctrine and Covenants must have a specific prohibition against women sitting on the floor in hospitals. I missed that part.

The fight that ensued lasted for days. It followed the familiar pattern - Tom screaming at me, with demands that I say I was sorry. I may have been a good Mormon, but I wasn't THAT good. My initial reaction was always the same... not only no, hell no. I didn't do anything wrong. After a while, (how long depended on how ridiculous the offense was, and how I felt at the time), I would cave in and apologize. This would start stage two of the fight. He would want to know what I was sorry FOR. I was supposed to recount the full litany of my sins. I would usually balk at this, too. By the time I was worn down enough to start recounting, I would no longer know, or care, what I was sorry for, which would only make it worse, because I would invariably miss something. Once this unpleasant little scenario had played out, the final stage would begin, which was WHY? Why had I done this?

Well, my response to THAT was "damned if I know!" That was not the correct response. Actually, there was no correct response. The final stage was nasty, prolonged, and unavoidable.

Two days after the beginning of this fight Tom came home from his night shift, woke me up to give me flowers and a card, and then started in yelling at me again. And I was the one who was crazy??? That next Sunday, after services, Tom called the Bishop and asked him to meet us at the church, because his wife needed direction. I was SURE that the Bishop, a seemingly reasonable man named Bob, would react with something along the lines of... "huh??" I was looking forward to being validated in my innocence. I was even hoping that this discussion would lead into a talk about treating your wife like an actual person. Instead, Bishop Bob looked at me and uttered words that remain burned into my memory - "Sister Thompson, do you really think it is appropriate to sit on the floor in a hospital?" At that moment I accepted utter defeat, and started to cry. The meeting ended with me accepting the direction to kneel down and pray for forgiveness. To this day, I hate the word "appropriate," and distrust men named "Bob."

Eventually, I took my G.E.D., and passed it with flying colors, with percentile scores that were so high that the examiner wrote on my test results, "Amazingly high scores! You should be doing something with these skills!" I took my entrance exams for Clearwater County Community College, and was told I could enter any program I wanted to. I started classes and was treated like an intelligent, gifted person. My English instructor liked my writing. The head of the math department, who was teaching one of my math classes, wrote our semester scores on the board next to the last four digits of our social security numbers, and explained how one person had skewed the grades for the entire class, because he graded on a Bell curve. One score was so much higher than any of the others that that one person and two others would get A's, but that one score had shifted the curve, so that people who would have gotten A's got B's, etc. I clearly remember sinking lower in my seat, hoping nobody would guess that it was me. I started standing up for myself and being more vocal. I went into the Electronics program and started a war with the head of the department.

I didn't really start the war, I just refused to concede. The two year program started with six women enrolled. One by one, they left, but I was not paying attention as to why. I was too busy getting A's and playing practical jokes. (One of those jokes involved an unused condom, unrolled and filled with Vaseline intensive care. It almost started a war). One quarter into the second year, there was only me, and one other woman left in the program. On her last day, she walked up to me and said "you're next." My response was "huh?" She told me the head of the department had driven out all the other women one by one, and I would be next. I did not believe her. The very next day, I was in class, not paying attention, because I never paid attention. The head of the department was teaching the class, and his lectures were notoriously boring. He knew I never listened, and he always ignored it. But today, he called on me and asked me to answer his question. My response was "huh?" (There is a pattern here....) He did not repeat his question, but said "Thompson, I just asked you a question. What is your answer?" My answer was "I'm sorry, Joe, but I haven't been listening to you for the last (I looked down at my watch theatrically) ten minutes, and I have no idea what you are talking about." He turned beet red, but went back to his lecture. From that moment the war was on. We jousted and fought, always with an audience, mostly in class, but sometimes not. It always ended with him turning red and me being smug.

In spite of my bumpy journey through the second year, I graduated with a GPA of 3.97, and went back to being a Mormon housewife, but no longer a very good one. In fact, I quit being Mormon, and one Sunday I flatly refused to go to church. My husband was now a Seventy, which is a big deal, and he was at a loss. He asked me how he was supposed to go to church without me - how would he answer the questions from our friends? I told him he could go to church if he wanted to. I wasn't going to try to talk him out of it, but I was not going any more. He asked what I was going to say when all of our friends started to call. I started to laugh, and explained how I felt. "Mormons don't actually make friends. They make checklists. I can tell you whose checklist I will be on - the Bishop, the Relief Society President, our Home Teachers, and my Visiting Teachers. Every one of them will have a box with my name on it. They will visit once, they will check the box, and that will be that." Terry told me I was wrong. I wasn't.

My visiting teachers, Elaine and Tara, came, and I told them that I no longer wanted them to come to my home as visiting teachers. If they wanted to come as friends, they would be welcome, but I did not want them to come again as visiting teachers. Elaine said "But Janet, you have so many friends at Church!" I answered "No, I don't. I have acquaintances at church, and I can have acquaintances at Safeway." She said I was wrong. They never came to my house again, but the next month I ran into Elaine at the home of a mutual friend. "Oh!" she said, "I'm so glad to see you! Now I can check you off my list and I will have 100% for my visiting teaching this month!" As Dave Barry says, you can't make this stuff up.

Excerpt Twenty Seven

Dr. Seuss Has An Attitude Crisis

Do I care?
I do not!
I do not give a whit!
A jot or a tittle
A lot or a bit!
I care not at all!
This place is a pit!
This job really sucks
And I don't give a shit.

Epilogue

"The reason we struggle with insecurity is because we compare our behind-the-scenes with everyone else's highlight reel."

~ Steve Furtick

By exposing a small sampling of people's "behind-the-scenes," my hope is that this book can help us all be more kind to others, and especially ourselves. Having a compassionate, understanding, forgiving, and patient inner dialogue with yourself is so important if you want to find happiness. I truly believe that this book can help us see that we are not alone in this world, whatever our struggles might be. We all experience pain and hardship even if everyone around us seems happy and "normal," and these stressful and painful situations are what make us grow as people. We wouldn't learn anything if our whole lives were roses and ice cream!

I hope you will learn something and find some sort of inspiration from these women's stories, even if it doesn't exactly mirror your own life experience. And next time you're feeling insecure, just remember not to be so hard on yourself, because we've all lived with self-doubt at various points in our lives.

With love,
L.M. Hughes

http://www.thesecretlivesofpeople.com